EMPOWERING WOMEN
Transforming Setbacks into Triumphs
on the Path to Success

I0559603

Get out
OF YOUR
OWN
DAMN
WAY

TRACEY LEE
along with 11 inspiring authors

TABLE OF CONTENTS

INTRODUCTION 5

Forward 8

Reclaim Your Freedom to Build Your Queendom
  By Shae Invidiata 14

Unleashing Dreams and Defying Doubters
  By Christina Singhal 47

Becoming Unshakeable: A Journey From Fear to Empowerment
  By Margaret Dennis 60

Awakened Healing: 7 Steps to a Renewed Life
  By Nubbia Quezada 80

From Breakdown to Breakthrough
  By Angeline Constantinou 98

Biohacking Your Way to a Better Life
  By Ariel Jarvis.. 112

How to Unleash Joy and Live Your Badassery
  By Melissa Trumble 130

The Midlife Metamorphosis: Birth of a Queenager
  By Sandra Mercer... 152

Trust, Rise and Thrive: A Path to Resilience, Healing and
Empowerment
  By Cheryl L Greenfield 169

Your Higher Self + Your Higher Goals = Your Key to Success
  By Debbie Calladine 186

Stepping Into Healthy, Fit and Vibrant ME: The Connection Between Mindset and Weight Release

By Leslie Gordon Christie 205

Jenn Iannuzzi 222

Tracey Lee 224

Conclusion 226

INTRODUCTION

It's your freaking time Bella!!!

To Get Out Of Your Own Damn Way!

Question is, do you know what it is you are getting out of your own damn way for?

I want to quickly share with you how the whole *Get Out of Your Own Damn Way* movement began.

I was invited to join another empowering successful woman in business at an All About Women's event to share a booth space with her.

The night before I thought about creative ways to connect with these women and I had no idea that what I came up with would have the impact it did.

Who knew that a simple full length mirror, with the words written in red lipstick across the top that said…

Look at me world, I'm getting out of my own damn way would call forward women of all ages to recognize where they were at in their life and knew deep down they were meant for more.

Women were stopping. They were staring at themselves and waking up to the idea they were in their own way. There were tears. Young girls brought their moms over to stand in front of the mirror and celebrate her ability to choose something better for her at that very moment.

It was a magical day and because of it, The Get Out Of Your Own Damn Way movement was officially born.

It was just the beginning.

I knew I wanted to create something big. Something that would have a ripple effect on a global scale. It also had to be an experience that would bring women together not only to be inspired, but also to inspire others. This meant a collective of women to come together and share their stories and believed in this mission. And in just a few short months I presented my vision to a zoom room full of incredible women who accepted my invitation to join me.

The global summit, Get Out Of HER Damn Way went from an idea I had sitting in my hotel room to becoming a reality. There were 20 powerful women speakers who got out of their own damn way and challenged themselves to do something bigger than they had done before, including myself.

I had never been to a summit, participated in a summit or championed an event like this. I just had a vision. If I had thought about it too long I would have talked myself out of being brave enough to make it happen.

There were three full days of interviews that brought out in all of us consistent laughter, tears, and every emotion in between. The stories shared were real, raw, and offered inspiration and truth with no hidden barriers.

This experience raised us all to a place where we knew we were meant for more and left a lasting impression on everyone who attended.

This book you are about to read is a compilation of every interview, story and golden nugget shared. There will likely be a part of you that relates to and connects with every woman's fear and failure that she shares. It's this vulnerability and truth that brings us closer together in sisterhood.

We were never meant to create and become our highest selves on our own. It takes a tribe, a village and others who have experienced the trenches you may be in right now. It's when we take down the false beliefs and the need to be perfect, we give ourselves permission to just be. That is what the Get Out Of Your Own Damn Way movement is all about.

I truly hope you gain some wisdom, courage, inspiration or new awareness from these incredibly powerful women who showed up for themselves and for women like you.

I am so grateful to all of the speakers, attendees, and the amazing support of others who came together to make this summit such a success. And now I get to bring it to you.

Find your cozy spot, curl up with your favourite beverage and feel the words on each page as if she is speaking directly to you.

Let's get ready to celebrate you and perhaps your next chapter in life.

And know it is never to late to get out of your own damn way.

Forward

Getting out of your own damn way. What does that mean to you? How would that look in your life right now? Take a moment to pause and really think about it. Can you see the parts of yourself, the beautiful parts, that are standing in the way of you experiencing those dreams you keep thinking about when no one else is around?

Maybe it's that sense of peace and calm you crave. Or perhaps the freedom to just get up and go on that weekend getaway you've been longing for. Or even the courage to invest in that exciting new opportunity that's been calling your name.

Maybe you have this incredible idea for a business, but the fear of all the things you think you lack has overshadowed any possibility of making it real.

Getting out of our own damn way starts with acknowledging the parts of us that have kept us safe, brought us to where we are now, and supported us in the past. But something powerful happens when we begin to pay more attention to the parts of us that are longing for more. Those whispers in your ear that say, "Why don't you try this? You'd be so good at that. You know you want to experience this… go do it."

But she's often drowned out, isn't she? The inner critic, the mean girl inside, tends to take over, and we stay stuck. We fill our days with what we're used to, what works for everyone else, finding comfort in the familiar. But then that other part of us returns, reminding us there's more out there waiting for us. And it just takes accepting that truth and beginning to move in a new direction.

I didn't start this journey until my late 40s, after years of ignoring the signs, the whispers, the nudges.

Like you, I've been shaped by life's challenges, those moments that force us to see things differently. The trouble is, we often go back to our old ways once the storm has passed. Or, sometimes, life doesn't give us that option, and we're pushed to make a change. That's what happened to me. The universe didn't give me a choice. My journey of getting out of my own damn way led me to take a chance on myself in ways I never imagined.

That's why I created the Get Out of Her Own Damn Way Summit. I had a vision, and when I shared it with a room full of women, they raised their hands to join me.

This summit was born from pure love, excitement, and a deep determination to make it everything it was meant to be. I invested in ways I never had before, all with the intention of creating an incredible experience for the women who stepped up to share their stories as speakers, and for those who attended and will continue to be inspired by it for years to come.

Choosing to do this summit wasn't logical. It wasn't the "right time." But my heart wouldn't let me say no. The energy and passion I poured into this summit over four months was like nothing I've ever experienced before.

And then, after the summit, everything changed. I was handed some tough lessons, ones that made me feel like the world was closing in, that I was alone, and that there was no way out. But I now call that stage of my life the RISE.

Because I chose to listen to the part of me that knew something my mind didn't. I let HER lead. I let her help me get out of my own damn way and rise above the circumstances I had created. Yes, we are the co-creators of our lives. There was something going on inside me that brought this reality to life.

And if I could see past the chaos, I could move through it, learn, grow, and become better.

Because that's what we're here for—to grow and to become better.

As I sit here in the early hours of the morning, writing this, I can honestly say I've gotten out of my own damn way. And I know I'll need to do it again and again. Because if you're like me, and you want to truly experience all that life has to offer, you'll have to keep taking those chances, stepping into the unknown, and trusting that deep down, you know this is what you're meant to do. The only thing stopping you are those parts of you that don't believe, that think you don't have what it takes, or that it won't turn out the way you imagined.

But here's what I've learned: when it doesn't turn out as you planned, it's because there's something better waiting. That thing, the one that's so right for you, can only come when the original plan doesn't work out.

This lesson—learning to trust on such a deep level that you keep raising your bar and becoming obsessed with how good you can get—is one of the hardest things to master. But getting out of your own damn way, this summit, and the next path you and I will take, is all about trusting.

This anthology is raw. It's conversational. It's me talking with the incredible women who chose to be part of the summit and who also chose to be in this book. Not everyone did, because things didn't turn out the way they expected, and they decided not to participate.

But what you'll find in these pages is a compilation of incredible stories, captured in the real, unscripted moments of our summit discussions.

You can also visit my YouTube channel to watch each of the interviews with these amazing women, each of whom offers unique gifts that might be exactly what you're looking for.

I want to express my deep gratitude for all the ups and downs, the highs and lows, and the love that was shared in the months leading up to and during the summit.

It was one of the most memorable and incredible experiences of my life, and I'm so blessed to share it with you.

I hope you enjoy the pages ahead. And I appreciate you for choosing *Get Out of Your Own Damn Way*. I hope it inspires you to do just that in your own life.

Sending you so much love and light.

I appreciate you.

Shae Invidiata

Shae + Co.
Impact Entrepreneur, Luxury Realtor,
Female Founder and Podcast Host

https://www.linkedin.com/in/shaeinvidiata/
https://www.facebook.com/shae.invidiata/
https://www.instagram.com/shaeinvidiata/
https://invidiata.com/
https://www.shaeandco.com/

Based in Costa Rica and Canada, Shae is an Impact Entrepreneur dedicated to creating positive change and building a legacy of significance. For 15 years, she has helped grow The Invidiata Team, a top real estate team in Canada, alongside her father, Christopher Invidiata. Shae has served as a Sales Representative, Manager of Operations, and Business Development at Invidiata Realty, contributing to its success with over $6 billion in sales and handling properties from $500,000 to $65 million

In 2010, Shae founded Free-Them, a leading anti-human trafficking non-profit organization in Canada. She has been recognized with the Queen Elizabeth II Diamond Jubilee Medal, numerous national media appearances, and TEDx Talks.

Shae is passionate about empowering women to achieve financial independence and become wealthy. Her mission is to inspire women to (re)claim their power and create a life of freedom, impact, and purpose.

Reclaim Your Freedom to Build Your Queendom

By Shae Invidiata

TRACEY & JENN MOMENTS

Jenn Iannuzzi: It's here. It's finally here. Welcome, welcome, welcome to the Get Out of Her Damn Way Summit, hosted by Tracey Lee.

I'm your emcee, Jenn Iannuzzi, and I'm just so damn excited to be here in all of this sisterhood, power, and brilliance. These three days promise to be packed with insight, wisdom, truth, and connection. And my job is to help you do what you do. With some helpful directions, a few bad jokes, and a whole lot of love and gratitude for all of you and all of the energy. So, who am I anyway? And why did Tracey ask me to hop in and hop on to fill this role? Unlike most of our speakers, I'm not a coach, but like all of our speakers, I'm a fierce champion of women. I'm a wife, mom to a teenage boy, stepmom, dog mom, daughter, insert all the roles. Professionally, I'm a marketing strategist, copywriter, and small business owner. I work full-time for an incredible company that creates software that helps companies do more good in the world. And I run my own marketing business that helps businesses tell the stories their customers need to hear. Like so many of you, I'm doing all the things! I met Tracey Lee when her husband stepped on our doorstep, like seven years ago, and asked for a cup of sugar. We've since spent hours chatting over Rosé and just being each other's cheerleaders. And I can't even begin to tell you how damn proud I am of my friend and mentor. To have witnessed her transformation in the past several years, well, it's nothing short of awe-inspiring. So when she told me a couple of short months ago that she had the vision to bring hundreds of women together in communities to share, learn, and grow, well, I just shook my head because, well, if you know Tracey, you just know that she was going to make this happen no matter what got in her way.

Are we fired up? Are you ready for the magic? Introducing our resident magician, host of "Get Out of Her Damn Way" and founder of the "Get Out of Your Own Damn Way" movement, Tracey Lee. With over 20 years as a women's fitness mentor and coach, Tracey stepped into her true purpose a few short years ago. She did the hard work, hired coaches to guide her along her journey, and invested in deep training. Today, as a women's business mindset coach and motivational speaker, she helps women overcome their fears and get out of their own damn way to take massive action toward their dreams. Tracey guides her clients to get clear on who they are, discover what they want, and break down the walls that keep holding them back. These women are now discovering their own purpose, running successful businesses, and stepping into their light and power. Tracey brings authenticity, passion, and her unique method and approach to our one-on-one and group-working clients. Never one to settle and always one to make a difference. She's launched even more ways to connect and support women, like right now. Tracey says that until you fully believe in your infinite potential, you can borrow her belief in you... It's my pleasure to introduce my friend and your host, the incredible Tracey Lee. Tracey, are you on mute? You might be on mute.

Tracey Lee: Yay, yay! My heart is exploding right now. Literally, I'm trying to contain my emotions because there's been so much anticipation. This is like a wedding day, Jenn. You need to walk me down the aisle.

Jenn Iannuzzi: Here comes the bride!

Tracey Lee: Oh my God, I've already been there, done that? I'm good, but first, I just want to say I am so grateful for this moment, for everything leading up to this moment, for having you here with me, Jenn, you know, when I asked you to do this with me, it's because I saw something in you that I wanted to pull out of you.

Jenn Iannuzzi: Are we supposed to cry this early?

Tracey Lee: I remember when we were on our little kayak last summer, and you were telling me that you were going to be emceeing at a massive event for your company with over 800 people. And you said to me, "Why is this happening, Tracey?" And you wondered if you were capable of doing it. And I said Absolutely, Jenn. Celebrating others is in your DNA.

You have incredible energy and a huge heart. When you combine that with your love to see others shine, people are drawn to you. I continue to see your gifts that you haven't seen in yourself. I knew your being a part of this summit was going to help pull out some of those gifts. So, I am honored to have you here to share your gifts and be our host for the next three days.

You are such a beautiful light in my life, friends forever. Right? And to all my incredible speakers. Oh my gosh, we've been on a journey for four months. This has been amazing, amazing, amazing, and I just don't know what to say. Well, I actually have a lot of things to say today. What I am going to say is, first of all, all of you women tuning in right now, tuning in over the next three days, you're friggin incredible. Don't let anybody tell you that you're not because we do not let that noise in from people who don't get you. You don't need anybody to get you.

You just need YOU to get you.

Jenn Iannuzzi: Oh, I'm feeling so coached right now. So, I'm sure everyone is feeling this right now, not just me. What a great start to the day, Tracey.

Tracey Lee: You know, the things we're going to share over the next three days, they're going to be so powerful. These women, these speakers that are showing up for you here, they've all had to get out of their damn way in so many ways. What this summit did was it lit a fire, a little fire in them. It ignited a little tiny flame that was in them to go bigger. They have stepped up, they have shown up, they have moved through obstacles, and they've become more awake to what it is that they are here to do than ever before. And they are showing up vulnerably and authentically. They're showing up powerfully for you all over the next three days. And my commitment to you is I will give you all of me for the next three days because this has been a dream I've had. This is only the beginning. Sitting here in my office thinking that this was just this little idea that I had back in May. And this idea has grown into reality. I didn't know how to do a summit. I've never been to a summit. I've never participated in a summit. I've never spoken at a summit. But here's what I share with you, ladies. I have my own summit. This is what we're doing. And you know why? I didn't want to just wait to take a seat at the table. I created my own damn freaking table.

Jenn Iannuzzi: Yeah, you did.

Tracey Lee: And these amazing women have sat down and joined me. And we can create our own table any day of the week. We don't have to wait for opportunities to come to us. We get to create the opportunities. I'm exactly like you. I started at ground zero in my business. I reset my life after crazy stuff happened, you know, losing everything financially, not wanting to be here, not on the right path, abusing myself in many ways, crawling out from under a rock because deep down I knew that there was more for me in my life. I am so honored to have you with me, Jenn. I am so honored to be here with all of you powerful women. I'm so honored to get to know you. I want to hear from you in the chat. Share whatever's coming up for you right now. How are you feeling? Why are you here? What do you want out of this day? What do you want out of these next three days? What kind of shift do you want to make in your life? Do you want to know you, your dreams, your ideas, your preferences all freaking matter? Do you want to realize how worthy you are?

Jenn Iannuzzi: Tracey, you're taking us to church already.

Tracey Lee: My body is vibrating, my heart is huge. I just feel I'm in the right place, and I hope that you guys do too. And Jenn, I'm honored that you are my wing girl for the next three days.

Jenn Iannuzzi: It's going to be fabulous.

Tracey Lee: And know that we're going to be dropping more information. We've got an amazing schedule. Every hour, you're going to get to meet speakers. Right after the speakers, after our interview together, you are going to step into a breakout session with each speaker. She's going to take care of you and be ready to answer all your questions. So stay tuned and don't miss a beat. We've got so many cool things going on. What are you showing me there, Jenn?

Jenn Iannuzzi: I'm showing you that I'm going to be taking that page, and that book is going to be filled with notes this week.

Tracey Lee: Oh, your journal. Yes. There's a beautiful journal, ladies. That's been created with so many heartfelt things in it. Things that are going to help you spend time with yourself, grow, and learn through the next three days. Grab your journal. You were sent an email with all the links in there. We're going to be dropping the links as well. If you haven't upgraded, you want to upgrade. You've been emailed the upgrade link as well. Your upgrade link gives you so many amazing things. You get all of the replays and lifetime access. And here's what I know. We learn by repetition. I need to hear things over and over and over again before they sink in. I've been studying the same things for years and now I'm starting to get it. I know my life's starting to get better. We've got gifts from the amazing speakers, beautiful gifts for you, and so much more. So, make sure you upgrade, and here's the biggest part about the upgrade.

Jenn Iannuzzi: This is huge. This is huge.

Tracey Lee: Eighty percent of what we earn through those upgrades, those funds are going to an incredible cause. A cause for people who don't feel they have a choice right now. They don't even have their voice to use right now. They're living in the deepest fear we can ever imagine. I'm talking about human trafficking. Free-Them is an incredible organization that's been around now, celebrating its 14th year. And we're so blessed to have our incredible keynote. She's been in the trenches in this space for 20 years. So that is the biggest reason to upgrade, to give back. Because what I know, and Tony Robbins says it all the time, the secret to living is giving. If you want to shift out of a low vibration, because maybe you're hiding out having a bad day, go and do something nice for somebody else, and you will be blown away at what happens next in your life. I am so honored to be here. I can't wait to share some of my stories with you before we jump on with our first incredible speaker. It's going to be powerful, it's going to be beautiful. Jenn, I appreciate you. I know you've got me this whole time, and I've got you.

Jenn Iannuzzi: Love you, girl.

Tracey Lee: Love you, love you, Jenn. Yay. And you'll see more of Jenn and Tracey because we're going to be around together a lot.

Jenn Iannuzzi: Sure.

Tracey Lee: We have some cool stories we'll tell you.

Jenn Iannuzzi: Do our thing!

Tracey Lee: So, we're going to do our thing, who's ready?!

Jenn Iannuzzi: I'm ready! And bye, Tracey!

Tracey Lee: Bye, Jenn. Amazing. Okay, I have a question for you, ladies, who here believes that they're in their own damn way, drop me a comment. I know I am. I know I'm in my own way. Who thinks that their life could get better if they got out of their own way? God knows I didn't even know I was in my own way. I had to become aware that I was in my own freaking way. And once I started to realize that, I had some serious choices to make, but here's the thing. If we are in our own way, and we do know that, then how did we get here? How did we get in our own way? We're intelligent women. Do you ever ask yourself powerful questions like that? How did I get here? How can we ever expect to change the fact that we're in our own way unless we start to understand why? And we're going to get to the root of this. Today, tomorrow, and Friday, we're going to get to the root of this stuff. You're going to leave with so many notes, so many awakenings, so many golden nuggets. We're going to get to the root of it so we can make a lifelong shift. Not just having a good month and changing a few things. I want to help you imprint something new into your life, mind, and heart. I want you to connect your mind and connect your heart. I want to help bring you a deeper connection with yourself. Why am I really here? Why do you think you're here? Why do we think we're here? Is it to just keep working hard, take care of your family, make enough money to pay your bills, maybe have some leftovers, so you can do something more for your family, go on vacation maybe, maybe buy that thing for your house. Is that why we're all here? To put our kids through school? So maybe they can do better than we did. Are we here to just keep doing the right thing, collect our pension, and then retire? Or did we come here in this lifetime to do something great? To be something great? To create something great? How good does that feel? Do you want to create something great in your life? Tell me if you can relate to this.

I used to live my life by a daily checklist. It was go, go, go, go. I celebrated the fact that, you know, I could multitask like nobody else could. At least, I thought in my head. I could run circles around people. I celebrated that shit. You know what? I was in a fight to control my life every single day. If I can get this done then I'll have time for that. And then when that happens, she'll be good, and I can drop her off, and then I'm going to go, and I'm going to do that. And then, and then, and then, and then, and then fill the space, fill the space, fill the space. And that mindset came from my past as a young girl trying to survive. You know, I was on my own at 17. I was orphaned at 17. I had to figure out life. I had a little sister. You know, we all have our crazy stories. We all have trauma. My trauma started at six. And this is why I was in this spiral of always thinking I had to just be in control. Checking off all the boxes gave me that. It was exhausting. So what I want to do with today in this beautiful time I have with you this morning, I want to share with you a story of how I got out of my own way, what I learned, and how it can help you do the same.

When I was writing down last night, "What story am I going to use?" There were so many: leaving the corporate world to become an entrepreneur, leaving a very toxic relationship after 18 years, and leaving a business that I liked for a business that I loved. I looked at all these stories, and I noticed something. I noticed that it was all about leaving something for something better. I noticed that there were all the sacrifices I had to make. There was a risk I had to take. And you know what? They all represented the same reason why I had stayed. The stupid F-word, fear. Fear kept me there. Fear kept me playing small. Fear kept me not seeing who I was, even believing in myself. My real get out of her damn way story isn't about what I did, ladies. This is about what I changed. Oprah Winfrey says, "The greatest discovery of all time is that a person can change her future by merely changing her attitude." It was time for me to make a trade. I had to trade something big because I wanted quantum leaps. I wanted a big change. I had to change and trade in fear for faith, control for surrender, believing things about myself, to believing in myself. I had to look at life through a completely different set of lenses. I took everything through a different set of lenses, and I mean everything. The catalyst to me accepting this new perspective, this new way of looking at my current circumstances, the lack of what was in my being, the lack of opportunities that I didn't see, the catalyst to all that, to acknowledging the biggest opportunity was shifting my attitude. There's a man named Earl Nightingale, you may know him, and he says, "If we take the attitude, 'we cannot do something, we generally will not do it.' What we accomplish or fail to accomplish is due to our attitude. We have to alter our attitude so we can alter our life." And you think, what is your attitude? Your attitude controls your bank account. Your attitude controls how you make decisions. Your attitude controls the standards that you set for yourself. Your attitude controls your discipline. It controls everything going on on the inside. And what's going on on the inside, you just have to look around because that's a direct reflection on the outside. And I know we know this. Maybe you don't know it. I didn't know it. When I started to realize it, I said, "Well, I need to know more, I need to understand this, I need to understand what this is all about, altering my attitude, altering my life." And when I started to do this work, it required me to make some massive sacrifices, sacrifices I had never made in my life before. Once I was aware of how attitude was impacting my life in a very negative way and understood the impact, I was left with a big decision. To stay where I was, to stay comfortable, to not rock the boat, to keep everybody else happy, or to take care of myself for the first time ever. Taking care of ourselves as women is really hard for us to do. We don't think we can walk through that door without everybody with us. That door of opportunity, that door where the unknown lives, the door where this summit lived for me, I had to set major boundaries with myself and my family to make all of this happen. I had to stretch myself beyond limitations. When you do this, you experience an incredible transformation.

Through this process, when I began to change my mind, I started to replace one habit at a time, one limiting belief at a time, one familiar story at a time. I had to change what I had always accepted for something else. I had to unlearn all this stuff, and I'm still in the process. Listen, I'm in the trenches, I'm in the fire with all of you. Every time you want to take yourself to another level, all the stuff comes flooding back into your life. But it does get easier because every time you experience it, you have evidence that you were able to do it. You stepped into the fire, and you didn't get burned. And if you did a little bit, you came out on the other side. When I was releasing these habits, limiting beliefs, and familiar stories, and changing what I accepted for myself, I raised my standards. I raised my desire. You know, we think that we don't get what we want because, you know, the opportunities aren't there. I didn't get the breaks. It's not about that. You have a weak desire. I had a weak desire for all the things I wanted in my life. We can want it all day long. I wanted, wanted, wanted, but nothing came to fruition. My desire was weak. I had to raise my desire. I had to raise my discipline in the right areas. Where was I focusing my energy on that wasn't serving me anymore? I had to raise my faith. I wrote down something today about faith. Faith is the substance of things hoped for the evidence of things not seen. But we must believe in it. I began to play in a different playground. It's fun over here.

I demanded and commanded something of myself in a way. I had never done it before. And what does this all do for me? Clarity. Can you imagine having more clarity in your life? What would that be like? What if you really woke up and you knew exactly who you were, what you wanted to do, and the obstacles? You could see them, and you could have an edge on yourself. What would that do for you? This brought me a deeper connection with myself. Why am I here? So when

I think about my vision, I cry, I feel it in my body, I feel it physically, I feel my heart get bigger. I acquired confidence that I never had before. Confidence to do this. I began creating something that was built from love. Fear will still come up. It comes up all the time. I started to understand why it's there, what it is, and how to render it useless. Because fear only happens when we leave the present moment. Think about it logically. The minute you set fear in your mind, you're thinking about something that could happen, or you're going back to the past. Will it happen that way? So, chances are it'll happen again. Or maybe you didn't have the support you needed, so why would you have it now? Maybe you didn't have the skills then, and maybe you did, but they didn't work out like they didn't work out for me. Tracey, I don't understand how it's going to work this time. We leave the present moment, we step into fear. Fear is ignorance. Ignorance is at the root of fear, and what I mean by that is you're scared. You're scared of what you don't know. So, it comes down to deciding: Do I want to be scared of what I don't know, or do I want to stay safe with what I do know?

Fear, do it anyway. Do it anyway because that's how you experience something. If you fail, it's okay. We only grow through our failures. We don't even grow through our successes. It's the failures that teach us and the more we know, the more experiences we have, the better we are. When I think about fear and I think about being scared, I'm doing it anyway. It requires surrender of the how. So many things in my life. Starting a business, leaving the corporate world, leaving a community that I've been around for 20 years that defined who I was. How could I step into something new? I had to surrender to the how, and the how represents a place that sits right in the middle of where you are and where you want to go. And right in this place is where control comes in. Here is where control and what we believe about ourselves come in. We need to control it, and we take in all the things we believe about ourselves. We fill that space. We fill it with what we know. Not what we don't know. We pull from that pool of the past, our personal inventory of fears, and what we have seen or heard from others. That's why we fill that space between where we are and where we want to go.

So if that's what we're filling it with, how are we ever going to get to that new place, that new life, that new career, relationship? When we fill that gap with all the things that aren't supporting our desires, we lose all our power. The power is always in the present moment. That is where all the power is. The present moment is what creates your future. You want to recreate your present moment. Recreate it right now. Think about what you want your present moment to look like. Write your present-moment story over the next three days. What do you want your present moment to be? How would your life be different? Who's the woman that's actually living that life? This is not easy work. This is the work I've been doing, and this is why I was able to completely change my whole life in 12 months. I was starting at Ground Zero, and every part changed; financially, relationships, my business, opportunities, powerful partnerships, my family life, and my health all shifted drastically in 12 months because of what I'm sharing with you.

If the present moment creates your future, what you fill that space with really matters. That space is in the middle of where you are and where you want to go. You want to fill it with something more. To do this, you've got to make a shift. You've got to trade in fear. You've got to trade that in for faith, for surrender to what is possible. Believe in yourself. If I had not made this trade, this summit wouldn't have happened. It wouldn't exist right now. If I didn't have the willingness to stretch myself, to stretch my belief for something greater than I'd ever experienced before, I would have stayed playing small. If I'd accepted all the excuses of not having enough money and what I had to invest to make this summit happen, the time it's going to take, the lack of experience, that maybe no one wants to come, I won't find speakers. If I'd have believed all that, none of this would have happened. This is all unknown territory for me. Start looking beyond your current circumstances. Raise your standards. If you've got things going on in your life that you don't feel good about, stop accepting. Start using faith to move you toward making powerful decisions. Fear is not where you want to birth your dreams from. Your vision deserves and needs you to be in the driver's seat of that vision, not other people's expectations of you.

I spent most of my adult life living up to other people's expectations. Can you relate? I didn't know how to take a chance on myself. I listened to the people that were the naysayers of the world. I listened to all of them. And I know we've heard stories like this. This isn't a new story that you've heard. But what are you doing about your story? You know, Mel Robbins always says, "No one's coming to save you. No one's going to tell you to get up to go work out. No one's going to tell you to make that phone call to that person." That could offer you something so incredible—a major shift in your life. No one's going to tell you to leave something that isn't serving you anymore. You have to be the one that's in the driver's seat making those decisions. And those decisions are risky. Those decisions are scary. Those decisions can have consequences. Those decisions can require boundaries to be set. Those decisions could maybe even affect another human being, but that's not your responsibility. Your responsibility is to rise up for yourself because when you rise up, and you start to tap into who you really are, I'm going to tell you right now, everybody wins. Everybody. And the people that don't want to hang around, they're not meant to be there. When your energy's in the right place, you attract exactly what you are. You are a magnet. You want to have magnetic confidence. The woman who leans into the excitement of what she doesn't know because that's where the joy of living exists.

Raise your standards. Accept new things about yourself and what you are capable of. If you don't, how can you expect anyone else to? It has to come from you first. Use faith to move you forward, to make powerful decisions. Gain an understanding of how the universal laws work, ladies. I talk about this in my training. The universal laws are what gave me elevated faith. We don't even understand how the universe works. We just hear these laws of attraction. You want to get rooted in understanding this because this is going to give you that little extra boost. You need to say, yes, I am going to do this in the outside world right now. It doesn't make sense. And guess what? It should never make sense in the outside world. When you make a quantum leap decision, that quantum leap decision is getting you out of that circumstance. Nothing should ever line up for you until you make the big decision. Most people run from it because they can't see it and, therefore, think it just doesn't make sense. The only sense is in your heart. That's what we want to get connected to—our hearts. Move away from the things that you believed about yourself that keep pulling you back into the past.

The past is over. It's over. You can't change it. It's not serving you anymore in any way. So why would you allow your past to destroy our future? It's not intentional, but we do this. Because it's a habit. You want to change your habits. You want to change your attitude. All these things, one at a time. Believe in yourself. That is the hardest work you're ever going to do because you are unlearning. You are going against the familiar. You are pushing against the stubbornness of the version of you that is doing everything to keep you safe. You're meant to soar. The first step can feel impossible right now. And that first step might be you just deciding to make a change. Maybe you're very successful in your life or your business right now. How good are you willing to get? That's my question for you right now. Write that down. How good am I willing to get? I want you to have an answer to that question by the end of these three days. You're going to fail. Lots of times. You're going to grow. You're going to get better and better and better. Don't settle for never knowing how great you and your life can be. Don't settle for always wondering. Don't settle for limiting yourself to just thinking of what you could have been. You are better than that. And deep down, you know this. That's why you're here right now. That's why you came to the summit. That's why you're watching this on the replay live. It doesn't matter. How good are you willing to get? That's the question I have for you.

I believe in you. You are powerful. You are loved. You are appreciated. You have everything you need inside of you. You are resourceful. You can find a way to do anything. Glendon Doyle says everything is figureoutable. It freaking is, ladies. Who is hell yeah right now for getting out of your own damn way? Who is a hell yeah? Woohoo! We have an amazing three days planned for you. And we have an incredible speaker coming up. Let's go!!!

Introduction

Introducing Shae Invidiata, a woman who has not only mastered the art of being the CEO of her own life but has also become an inspiration to many. My connection with Shae dates back several years, when she became my client in a wellness business. From the moment we met, there was an undeniable, energetic connection, and we both knew we were destined to do something great together. Today, I'm thrilled to share a glimpse of Shae's journey, one that is marked by bold choices, a deep sense of purpose, and an unyielding drive to live life on her own terms.

Shae's story begins in Oakville, Ontario, where she grew up surrounded by a family that instilled in her a strong sense of values and a passion for creativity. Art was her favorite subject in school, and this early love for creativity has been a guiding force in her life. Today, she finds herself splitting time between Costa Rica, Toronto, and Oakville, embracing the complexities of a life lived across borders. Wherever she is, though, Shae brings with her a spirit of adventure and a deep connection to the world around her.

One of the defining traits of Shae is her boldness. When asked whether she is more cautious or bold, her answer is clear: "Bold, if you can't tell." This boldness is reflected in the way she approaches life, whether it's her love for fresh food over fried or her preference for cannonballing into the pool rather than dipping a toe in first. Shae doesn't do things halfway—she's all in, every time.

Her bold approach to life is also evident in her choice of vehicle. If she could afford any car, it would be an F1 McLaren—a car that, much like Shae, is designed for speed, precision, and making a statement. This same precision and dedication can be seen in the way she tackles challenges, always opting to learn by watching others' mistakes and then doing it better herself. Her father, whom she considers her hero, has clearly been a guiding influence in her life, teaching her the value of learning and perseverance.

Despite her fearless approach to life, Shae is also deeply introspective. When asked what makes her hopeful, she answers, "Humanity." This hope in people, in our collective potential to do good, drives her to make an impact wherever she goes. Whether it's through her work, her relationships, or simply how she carries herself, Shae is committed to making a difference.

When it comes to her personal life, Shae embraces the simple pleasures—like enjoying cheese and red wine for dessert or savoring avocado toast with eggs for breakfast when she's not fasting. And while she admits to regretting spending money on books she doesn't end up reading, it's clear that she values experiences, like the pottery she recently made with her three-year-old niece, over material possessions.

Shae's love for the water, her passion for travel, and her commitment to living boldly all point to a woman who is not just the CEO of her life but the architect of a life filled with purpose, creativity, and unrelenting passion. She may have once thought about changing her name to Joey from *Full House* when she was younger, but today, Shae knows that her name, much like her journey, is uniquely hers—and she wouldn't have it any other way.

As you prepare to dive into Shae's interview, I encourage you to embrace the boldness and creativity that she brings to everything she does. You're about to be inspired, challenged, and uplifted by a woman who truly lives life on her own terms. So grab your coffee, take a deep breath, and get ready to meet Shae Invidiata—a force of nature who is here to remind you that you, too, are powerful, loved, and ready to take on the world.

INTERVIEW

Shae Invidiata: Good morning!

Tracey Lee: Oh, yeah, how awesome is this?

Shae Invidiata: Oh, man, well, there are not too many things I love more than speaking to women and being in a group of great company of women. So this is such a fantastic way to start the middle of the week. It's hump day today.

Tracey Lee: Yeah, it's hump day, and let's re-energize, right? Let's refocus, re-energize, let's rise up.

Shae Invidiata: Thanks for having me here, I was backstage listening and, of course, Tracey, when you gave me the call, right from the beginning. As you mentioned, we connected on water. That's actually what united us together was upping the quality of our water. And since then, it's been such an incredible journey of how we're going to work together. What can we do together? How can we make an impact? And so when Tracey gave me the call to say, "Hey, would you come and be the keynote speaker?" It was an instant fuck yes. Because if you don't feel it right down below then why are you showing up? Why are you doing it? Right? Time is too precious. So, it's a non-renewable resource. So, we have to be careful and intentional with what we're saying yes to.

Tracey Lee: Yes, yes, absolutely. And what we say yes to, we attract more of that, right? So, it matters more than we realize. And this is a habit that I had to get into, you know, is embodying the word yes from a place of my heart, not just a place of what I thought I needed to say yes to. So, today, you and I are talking about reclaiming your freedom to build your queendom. Like, I love queendom. We've got one of our speakers that's wearing a crown, I'm pretty sure, today. So, being the queen, let's just talk about queendom for a minute, Shae. What is that?

Shae Invidiata: You know, to me, when you are in your queendom, it's really knowing your value. It's knowing your worth, number one, right? When you talk about putting on that crown, it's your fortress. It is a life that you have built that you absolutely love, and you're willing to guard it at all costs, you know? So whatever your mission is, you're so clear on what it is you're doing, and you're willing to guard it at all costs. Things that come your way might be attractive, right? You might want to say yes to it, but if it doesn't align with your mission, if it doesn't align with your queendom that you're building, you got to guard that, you know? So I think that's how I see it for myself. And there's so much power that resides within your queendom. So many women need this. The most beautiful part is that the world is waiting for you to step into what you are meant to be doing in your life. So, we're going to talk a little bit about this today. You know, I want to also just share because I have such an interesting background here.

Tracey Lee: I want you to tell a little bit about your story first. Let's do that. Just something so these incredible souls reading this can understand who the heck you are and how she got to where you are in life. What's been the inspiring highlights of your journey? Shae, you have so many stories.

Shae Invidiata: I do have so many stories, including the one this morning, which is so wild, but it's great. I'm literally sitting in somebody's loft above their garage right now, okay? And there's a story there, we can come back there, but this is not normal life for me right now. But this is the power, I always think about things like this. This is the power when you know you're doing something incredible and that you are aligning your mission, you know, sometimes, the other powers that be try to pull you away from that because what you're doing is so important. And so rather than get frustrated, it's like, okay, I see you. I'm acknowledging that and I need to pivot because what I have to say, what I need to do, what my mission is, is so needed. It's so powerful and so strong that I'm just going to not be upset. I'm going to look at that and go, well, that's funny. So this is part of why I'm in this garage this morning.

Tracey Lee: I need to know why. I'm literally dying to know why.

Shae Invidiata: Okay. So, you know, I'm in Costa Rica full-time right now. I have properties in Toronto, but I don't have a primary. So, you know, I'm visiting with my mom. I might visit with another girlfriend of mine. So I'm at my mom's place. And yesterday, last night, she said the fire alarm testing is going off in the building tomorrow, starting at 9 am. I'm like, you've got to be kidding me. Of all days, 9 am. We all know fire alarms, there is no hiding. It's going to be in the unit. It's going to be in the building. And I'm like, I can't do this to all the women or Tracey.

So I called my dad. Can I come to your place? He's like, my cleaners are there tomorrow morning. They can't rearrange their schedule because she's got a daughter with special needs, and it's very complicated. Believe it or not. So that was a hard no. Then I was like, okay, well, I'll go to our office, nope, there is a team meeting this morning. Can't do it. Going to be lots of people there and a lot of noise. I'm like, shit, what am I going to do? I was prepared to be doing this from my car, okay? I am still tethering my phone to my laptop because as I said, I'm in a room above a garage that does not have wifi. So I called a girlfriend of mine. I was like, this was at 11 o'clock last night. I'm like, I know this is a really strange request. Can I maybe use that room that you showed me? So, I've got like a bed if I need to lie down, I've got some workout stuff there. But this is part of recognizing I could either have been derailed this morning and be completely stressed that my background doesn't look as pretty as Tracey's. I knew what I was showing up in! And I was like, no, this is part of understanding what it is you're protecting. This is part of my Queendom journey this morning. So that's my funny moment, okay?

I grew up in an entrepreneurial business household, coming from Oakville. It's also known as an affluent community. So, I've worked alongside many different CEOs and executives of many different organizations and corporations over the years within the real estate realm. And I've always, from a young age, challenged the status quo that you have to wait for it to come true. You've climbed the corporate ladder, or you've hustled the nine to five, or you've started a business, and maybe you're burnt out, or you've just been grinding for so long. You have the kids and you're at this later point in your life where now you may have more time, and that's the system that has made us believe that that's when we start giving back. You know, that's when we can start enjoying life. That's when we start doing the things we really love. And from a young age, I was like 19 being like, well, I don't want to wait till I'm older to make an impact. I think you can do both at the same time. And if you're telling me I have to wait until I'm older to start having fun or enjoying what I'm doing. Like, I might as well just leave this place now. What is the point, right? What is the point if the journey to where your destination is is not enjoyable, is not fun. And so I was lucky that I learned some of these life lessons in my early 20s, and I began to weave them into the fabric of my business and what I was doing.

So simultaneously, I started out my real estate career, and I founded Free-Them at the same time, which I don't necessarily recommend doing both those things at the same time, but you could kind of do it like this, you know, start with something that brings something else along. I went for both at the same time. And, you know, through that, we've made an incredible impact in our nation. As Tracey mentioned, it's an organization that fights human trafficking here in Canada and abroad. We focus on all things to do with prevention, awareness, education, legislation, fundraisers, speaking engagements, and talking to the young ones. That's my favorite. I love going to high schools and speaking to the kids. And not just talking to the kids, but also permitting them to pursue their dream for exactly what I said, right? Like, they can make a difference right now. And children are so impressionable, and they believe you with what you tell them. And so I love going in and saying, you can totally do it. If I can do it, you can do it. You know, along the way I've just become a really big advocate for my health and strongly believe in chemical-free and toxic-free living, and that's not just about what we eat. The water we drink and what we're putting in our bodies also has to do with our minds, right? We're assuming what we're thinking about, our thoughts, all of these things. I'm still on this journey as we all should be like students, but it is one of self-mastery to really eliminate the toxic load in our bodies.

You know, you mentioned in my introduction that I'm an ex-planter, even though I'm not an expert. What the hell is that? So, I had breast implants for 11 years. I had two sets over those 11 years. I removed them on March 2, 2022. And so that is the term ex-planting, which has made me an ex-planter. Because I just had a really honest conversation with myself about living this chemical-free life, toxic-free life, yet you have these toxic, you know, carcinogen, neurotoxin products chilling in your body. I shouldn't say chilling, but cooking in your body at 87 degrees. I had a very hard conversation with myself, but the decision was simple. And so that's what I say. It was the simplest decision of my life to remove them. I still love my implants even now. And there are many days when I'm like, I wish I had them. But I value my health more. And that's not to say that women who have them or learn about BII breast implant illness. And it's just learning, the more we know, the better we can do.

Tracey Lee: I remember when you and I spoke about reclaiming your freedom, like going to Costa Rica, doing your ex-plant, all of those things, I feel you were already very successful. I think that's important for women to know: It's not about I've had my success, and now I'm good. It's about what's next. What's the next door that I'm willing to walk through? I remember when you shared that with me. You were telling me your surgery was coming up, and we're just building our relationship. We had these beautiful conversations on the phone. But I really feel that those moments were defining moments when you chose to leave, you know. And create something outside of where you were with your family because when you're in a family business, you're in it like it's all-encompassing, right? You had the inner strong desire that you knew you were being called to do something different, and you listened to her. She shared with you a new opportunity that you could start to decide, okay, am I going to do this? And those are all big moments. I feel that was a really defining moment for you to reclaim your freedom, Shae.

Shae Invidiata: It was and I went on to develop a whole thing for women who have ex-planted, and it was called Reclaim Ex-planter Embodiment Retreats. And the intention is to get on the journey of coming home to yourself, right? Because anytime we make decisions or lack thereof, we let somebody else be in control of our health, be in control of our mind, of our relief. Maybe we're stuck in a job that we don't love, that doesn't excite us. You're giving a piece of yourself out in all these different areas, and I took my healing journey on that seriously, knowing that there were so many other women who did not realize that there was a journey to be on, for starters, okay? There are different healing tools and modalities that will help you to come home to yourself and re-welcome your feminine, and re-welcome her with it. So, I really started to incubate on this word 'reclaim' and look at our foundations, and this is part of what we're talking about today. I think it's amazing, actually that this is the topic that is setting the stage for these next few days. And when you first asked me about what do you want to share? I really took it to heart because this is the foundation piece. And so, it is so important for us to start to analyze and look at where we have actually given away our power. Where have we given pieces of ourselves? Whether it's because we feel pressured, maybe it's an expectation of a family member or a partner or a sibling, friends, whatever it is. But in order to get out of your own way, right, it is necessary for us to be reclaimed. So we have a solid foundation. You have to hold things in and go, "Okay, that's no more." If you don't have a solid foundation, you might be able to do what you want to do for a little bit, but you're going to start getting pulled in a different direction because you've not actually called back in your power into these different areas of your life. And sometimes, it is physical. A lot of the time, it is emotional. You know, for me, it was also mental for what I was going through, even though this was such a physical thing, there was so much mental that needed to be addressed. But to recall your freedom in life, to be able to do what you want to do, to really step into what I call being the CEO of your life, it starts with taking radical responsibility for everything in your life right now. There's nobody else to blame. Not that father who pissed you off or hurt you, you know, that spouse you ended up leaving or he left you, all of these hard things in our life, it's about taking radical responsibility and recognizing there's nobody else to blame for where you are in your life right now.

Tracey Lee: Yeah.

Shae Invidiata: And that's not easy. I can use my dad. We all have relationships with our parents, and some days or some years are better than others. I mentioned in my Rapid Fire that my father is my hero. I've gone through some really challenging times over the past few years of my life with my dad, and my relationship with him has changed. It's really easy for me to hate or not like or be uncomfortable or be mad in anger and resentment, and I've gone through all of that. That's the human response, but I'm also at a point in my life where I thank him for everything good because it shaped me. Everything I've not liked has also shaped me and my today. You don't always need to enjoy the process. You don't need to say that it was fun. You honor it and acknowledge it was shitty. It's hard. It's hurtful. It's ugly, whatever it is for you, but you wouldn't be who you are without the polarity. You wouldn't be able to enjoy the joy. You won't be able to enjoy the good without the opposite.

And so, stepping into these next few days where you're going to hear from incredible speakers coming in with powerful messages. Can you take a few moments? If you've downloaded the journal, or if you haven't done it, take a piece of paper or anything and just make it. Promise to yourself that today you're going to start with taking radical responsibility for your life because you want to build a new foundation. You're calling yourself home. You're calling her in so that she can come out and shine. And so we are going to build a new foundation, which is so freaking exciting and is so empowering. And knowing that from this moment forward, you get to start making your own decisions. And when you do that, even if they're the wrong ones, there's a lot of freedom in that. Because you're the one, you're betting on yourself, and then you can pivot, you can correct your course because you're not relying on anybody else to do that for you.

Tracey Lee: Yep, power is right, that's all the power.

Shae Invidiata: Big time. 100%.

I think the foundation is key, and you know we have cracks in our foundation. And those cracks are up to you to fill.

Shae Invidiata: Yes. Yes. It is.

Tracey Lee: It's up to you. No one's going to come and fill them for you, and when you're going to have other cracks that pop up, and you're going to fill them. This is the process, like you said, we just have to accept that this is part of the process you can't get around it even if you think you're going to play it safe and not step into your power. It is going to catch up with you because either life throws you against the wall and you're forced to start filling those cracks in, or you make a decision and be the CEO of your life, and you do it yourself.

Shae Invidiata: 100%. And that's where you get us, literally, put the line in the sand, you can fill your cracks, you can change the foundation. But when you choose to make better decisions, when you choose to change, your life changes, right? That's how it goes. Instead of blaming other people, waiting for somebody to come and save you or somebody to come and help you, it's going, no, I'm in control of my own happiness. I'm in control of my own destiny. And I am capable. It is possible. And I have the tools, more than you realize. And it's really time for women, especially, to rise up into their power, rise up into their worthiness, and live life on their own terms. The only way you can do that is if you start taking ownership. It's about looking at where you're vulnerable in your life. You know, I think about a lot of women in the past few years. We've all been challenged with different protocols or measures or mandates, whatever it is that is demanding for us to do or not do certain things. And you should really understand why you're doing those things. And if you do not, that's where you need to pump the brakes and go, where am I vulnerable? If I got sick today, who would I rely on? Do I rely on myself? You know, I'm the essential oil queen. I never have an oil that's not in an arm's reach of me. That's what I always say, okay? And so right here I have the oil "peace" that I put on before this. Are essential oils the be all and end all for your health? No. There are times when Western medicine absolutely plays a role. But there's a lot of times when, I mean, I don't rely on the system. I know how to handle my health. And that's something I have been dedicated to that practice for over 10 years of my life. So, it's a journey.

Tracey Lee: Yeah.

Shae Invidiata: Finances are another one. How many women do not understand the language of money? They don't have financial literacy. They don't know what it is to invest. These are areas where you become exposed, and you have to outsource your trust, whether that's to a man in your life, your partner, your husband, or whoever it is. Maybe it's to the government expecting a pension and a paycheck, whatever it is. Now, having a man in your life who's great at finances is not a bad thing. That's a fantastic thing. If you have a pension—wonderful, amazing—that's great for you. But what if that husband left tomorrow, passed away, circumstances changed, your job got deleted, whatever it is, so ask yourself, where am I vulnerable in this? Could I handle myself? Could I make money for myself? How do I make money? Where are my investments? So these are different areas and different pillars in our lives where we need to look at where do I need to reclaim because we don't have freedom in that.

Tracey Lee: Yeah, yeah.

Shae Invidiata: Right?

Tracey Lee: I think we don't like to do that because it makes us feel ashamed. It makes us feel vulnerable. It makes us feel like we're in comparison mode. It is the ickiest feeling, and we run away from anything painful. We run to pleasure, and we run away from pain. But the thing is, if you can just get over that hump and that's when you need support, you need the right people. If you're in a certain situation right now, you've got to look at all the elements of your environment. If your environment isn't supporting you to move on another journey, you're going to want to sit down and be the biggest advocate of that part of your life. I'm going to tell you that your best friends are only thinking about themselves. You have to understand that you've got to step into being the most important person in your life because then the people connected to you will be taken care of in so many different ways. Just get off the whole bus of victimhood. You're not a freaking victim. You are an incredible, powerful woman. And you are resourceful. You may not know and find out. And that's what this is about. After the summit, we're giving you a network of women to stay connected with, learn, and grow with. This is a container of safety from a place of no judgment, no blame, no shame, for community, for excellence, for authentic, for vulnerable, for inclusive.

And inclusivity is a huge part, right? And I know that's who you are to share. You're an inclusive soul, right? You don't leave people out, you bring them in. We're doing the freedom movement within this summit because those people don't have a voice. They, actually, do feel very powerless right now. And so we're showing up to help serve them. It's amazing. I want to ask you, what are your top CEO principles? Because we keep talking CEO. What are those top three principles?

Shae Invidiata: So, there is a number, but I would say there are about eight to ten, but looking at my top three, and we've just kind of touched on that a little bit, but the first one for me starts with mindset. The second is leadership, and the third is financial literacy. And I'll break this down for you a little bit. We've all probably been an employee at some point before. I even break it down because I want to talk about the energy of what it means to be a CEO and how that feels. So, I know women are tuning in today who are not CEOs and have never been a CEO. Maybe they've never even worked for anybody. Maybe you've been a stay-at-home mom from the beginning, or you jumped right into entrepreneurship. And so you've always just been you alone. But I know there are a lot of other women who have been employees. Maybe you've been in management, maybe you've been higher up. But think about working for somebody else for a moment and think about what that feels like. If you close your eyes and you're an employee, I don't want to say just an employee, but you're an employee and a company, okay? And how that feels, the day in and day out, sometimes people notice you're there, sometimes they don't. Your higher-up managers, some know your name, some might not. There is this energy that you take on as an employee around, maybe your value and worth, or the importance of your role. And part of climbing that corporate ladder, as an example, is as you become quote-unquote more important, you go up that ladder. There's a new energy. There's a new feeling, a new persona that you embody when you become a manager, and when you go higher up, you become a regional manager or director, and then you become an executive.

Again, of course, it's partly the ego as well, but there is this energy where you feel more confident, more assured of yourself, and you're given more responsibility. You're becoming more in the driver's seat. I want every woman here this morning to close their eyes and feel what it's like to continue as I am talking, to feel that you are at the top of that ladder. You are the only decision-maker; people come to you looking for direction, and you might have guidance and advice. But, ultimately, it's your call, and it's your say. If somebody else makes a different recommendation or they have a different opinion, yours still trumps anything else. There is a confidence that exudes you above most other people who are in that company because you're the one who's driving the ship. You're the one that's driving the bus. You're the one that's driving that car. You're the one leading the company. And so, naturally, there's this badass attitude and this badass feeling that is inevitable. You can't help not feel that because you know you're running the show. It starts with this energy that then goes into your mindset. This is where I go with the number one thing about being a CEO, which fundamentally starts with your mindset. You might not be leading anything right now. You might not have a company that you're running, but you need to embody it now to become first. Your future self is waiting, she's there, and she's a freaking badass, but it starts in your mind. So you have to feel that energy and start to shift your mindset and thoughts, right? Your resilience, letting go of the weight of the opinions of other people. I've heard many other people say it in different ways, but other people's opinions of me are none of my business. No, you have to learn how to throw that off because if you're constantly concerned about the opinions of other people, you'll never be able to rise up. You won't because the higher you rise, the more spectators come out with their own opinions. I always say you should never ever take advice from somebody who has not done what you want to do, and it's not where you are if they are not in the ring fighting the same fight. You invite them as a spectator and give them tickets to front-row seats. Yeah, and you say thank you for coming. So great for you being here, but you don't listen to them. You only are paying attention to people who are in the ring and who have actually already won and are doing bigger things than you.

Tracey Lee: Don't you find, Shae, that the higher up you go as well, that there are fewer opinions, and there's more support? You know what I mean. I find people who are so opinionated are so because they're in fear, they're sharing that, and they're spreading that to you like an infectious disease. Whereas someone who's truly, truly in their power, they just want to support.

Shae Invidiata: Totally. I think there are two sides to that. This speaks to the testament of the circle in which you choose to surround yourself, Tracey. As you are climbing up your own ladder, as you're rising up into the CEO ship of your life and your mission, you are going to have people that are going to try to keep you from doing that because that's our natural defense mechanism. That's a fight-or-flight state. Sometimes, they're not doing that because they're jealous or don't want to see you rise. Sometimes, those people are real, and they should be cut out. Oftentimes, it's the safety mechanism that goes off in all of our brains, especially for those people who are living in more fear or doubt, right? I think it speaks to the circle in which you've chosen to surround yourself.

It becomes so important that there are people we have loved dearly along the way that are going to now take a different spot in the ring, if you will. And sometimes, that inner circle, they move to the outer circle, and that's super important. Because yes, the people who are championing you, who are supporting you, those are the people who you want to keep in your closer circle. And they're the ones who want to see you rise. They're the ones that are going, yes, I will show up for you in any capacity. So we need to be mindful of that. Right?

The second is around that leadership component. Some women get really freaked out when you use the word leader, like why, I'm not a leader, I don't know what to lead. How to lead. All day long. I think they get freaked out. Let me tell you a secret. Being a CEO is around self-leading. This is around leading yourself. And when you learn how to master it, it's always an ongoing process. That should be the goal because as you are evolving, your desire and your vision are going to expand. As you're evolving to become the person that you want to be and the goals you want to achieve, you're going to start seeing new things. It's going to be this moving target if your goal is to continue to evolve and grow. As you learn how to better lead yourself, trust your intuition, and lean on yourself, you're a living example that is going to inspire others to start taking their own responsibility in their lives. You'll become a leader without even realizing it.

I encourage each of you today to not worry about all of a sudden needing to come up and speak somewhere or start using your platform around leadership. No, this is around you and becoming the master of who you are. You can even forget about the word leadership, but I'm using it here for clarity because that is what you're doing. This is learning how you take charge of your own life. And the more you lead yourself, like I said, you're going to become an example to others who are going to be inspired to start doing things the way you're doing them.

Tracey Lee: That's the ripple effect. And it's beautiful. That's the thing. I feel truly that we have a responsibility to ourselves. The real reason why we came into this world is to actually clear away the shit, fill the cracks, put our big girl pants on, tighten our ponytail, and do this right. This is why we need women's circles and have this holistic space for taking care of ourselves emotionally, behaviorally, mentally, and spiritually. We need help in all those areas like finance, relationships, health, and mindset. All of these things. We need it all in order for us to truly keep rising up. That is hard work. It's not grinding through your job. That's the hard frickin' work. And when you just even a little bit decide to give yourself an extra 1% boost and show up for yourself, take a chance on yourself, 1% more. You will enjoy something different in your life today. And you guys attracted this invitation to come to the summit. Like, know that that happened. I attracted amazing speakers. I attracted Shae into my life. God has big plans for us, Shae. And I know that we're just leaning in. We lean in and get in the habit of leaning in instead of running away. And every time you do that, it doesn't necessarily get easier because the leaning in can be greater and have more risk to it. There's more unknown, but you do start to create the evidence, you build the confidence, and you start to step into natural leadership roles because you're like, holy crap, this is what I'm doing. And you start to learn stuff about yourself. It's foundational to your being. The CEO of your freaking life and reclaiming your power, right?

Shae Invidiata: Totally, hundred percent, hundred percent.

Tracey Lee. I love you. High five to you all day long, sister. You're amazing. My heart is so full right now. Thank you, thank you,

Shae Invidiata: I love you, Tracey. I'm really excited to just be a participant, too, and soak in all of the goodness with the rest of the community.

Tracey Lee. Let's do it. Amazing. Okay.

To watch Tracey Lee's interview with Shae Invidiata, scan the QR Code below.

Christina Singhal

Christina M Singhal, LLC
Life Empowerment Coach

https://www.linkedin.com/in/christina-singhal/
https://www.facebook.com/ChrisMsing
https://www.instagram.com/chrismsing
https://linktr.ee/christinasinghal
https://soulspiritcoaching.com/

"Christina - Inspiring Others to Persevere and Achieve Their Goals"

With over 23 years of personal experience overcoming obstacles and setbacks, Christina is dedicated to inspiring individuals to never give up and to continue pursuing their goals and dreams.

As a former Registered Nurse in the South-African Defense Force, Christina gained valuable experience while working in the community in South-Africa and across London and the USA while exploring diverse cultures.

Known for her ability to "bring people together" and foster a sense of community, Christina is now a Life Coach, helping others improve their relationships, enhance their health, and find meaning in everyday life.

Join Christina on this exciting journey filled with fun and contagious energy!

Unleashing Dreams and Defying Doubters

By Christina Singhal

Introduction

Introducing Christina Singhal, a seasoned DreamBuilder Coach from the Notable Brave Thinking Institute. Christina's passion lies in igniting souls and guiding individuals, particularly married women, toward lives filled with joy and authenticity. With an innate ability to shatter limiting beliefs and empower others to stand tall regardless of their circumstances, she's here to help us break through our self-imposed barriers and soar to new heights.

Christina's journey began with her first job at Truett's, a store in South Africa, where she started to develop her strong work ethic and love for helping others. Her favorite month is December, a time filled with the joy of the holiday season, which aligns with her warm and caring nature. Summer is her favorite season, reflecting her vibrant and energetic spirit, and she loves spending her time on the beach playing volleyball, a sport that allows her to combine her love for the outdoors with her competitive streak.

Her favorite animal is a dog, a loyal and loving companion that mirrors her own values of love and connection. Blue is her favorite color, symbolizing calmness and reliability, qualities she brings into her coaching practice. Christina's favorite food is chocolate, a sweet indulgence that she enjoys amidst her busy life.

Christina's favorite word is "I Can," a mantra that encapsulates her belief in the power of positive thinking and self-empowerment. On the flip side, she hates hearing the word "Why," as it often signifies doubt or hesitation.

Family is central to Christina's life, and she texts her daughter the most, staying connected and supportive. Her favorite age so far has been 40, a time when she felt truly in her element, combining life experience with her passion for personal development. When it comes to lazy dinners, pizza is her go-to choice, a simple pleasure that brings comfort after a long day.

Christina is married to a tall, dark, and handsome man, and together they have two teenagers who keep life exciting. Although she recently lost her beloved dog, she looks forward to welcoming a new furry friend into their home this summer. For Christina, love always takes precedence over friendship, and happiness is far more valuable than money. Dogs are her preferred pets, reflecting her love for loyalty and companionship.

The best advice Christina has ever received is simple yet profound: "Just do it." This advice has fueled her approach to life, encouraging her to take bold steps and embrace challenges. She wishes she had learned about personal development sooner, as it has become a cornerstone of her work and personal growth. Her biggest fear? Sharks—a reminder of the unknown and unpredictable in life. She also admits to speaking too fast and sometimes feeling intimidated, which she views as her biggest flaws, but these challenges only add to her authenticity.

When it comes to holiday food, Christina has a special place in her heart for Fate cook, a traditional South African dish that brings back memories of home and family. Through her work, Christina Singhal is committed to helping others build lives filled with joy, authenticity, and boundless possibilities.

INTERVIEW

Tracey Lee: Oh my gosh, how are you doing?

Christina Singhal: I'm doing fine. I have been ready, I'm so ready, I'm so excited. I want to be prepared for this and look at this, Tracey. It's amazing. You did this.

Tracey Lee: So fun, right? Starting with an idea, I just put my laser beams out there and attracted you like we had never met before. How did you find this whole experience? Like, where did you come from? Let's tell them, let's tell the group how this all happened because I think it's important in terms of we show up in our power, just like Shae was talking about, really standing in that and creating that foundation, and all of a sudden we start attracting new things into our life as I attracted you and you've attracted me.

Christina Singhal: This is the power of the phone. So, I was scrolling on Instagram with one of my fingers like, I'm never going to be a scroller, but I did scroll. I saw a topic, Get Out of Her Damn Way, and I'm like, wow. My antenna went up. What the heck? So I started reading about your upcoming invitation for speakers. That's where I started. See, that's where my life with you started. I sent you an email just to find out more. And then you asked, "Do you want to sign up?" Yes, I am. I may as well just give it a try. This will be my first speaking engagement, and it's been an amazing experience so far.

Tracey Lee: Yeah, we've had a really fun four months together preparing. We've been doing our thing and getting to know each other on such a deep level. I really have gotten to know you in so many different ways. I lit a little fire under you, and you are incredible and what that's done is it's allowed you to really show up and stand in your power like you're the advocate for the life you want to live. You know you're stepping into such an incredible place of really helping other women unleash their dreams and defy doubters in their lives. And, yes, I want to ask you what Unleash Your Dreams is. What is that exactly? Let's jump right into this conversation.

Christina Singhal: Okay, do you know *The Croods*? I don't know if you saw *The Croods* where they were yelling, "Release the baby! Release the baby!" And they let that baby go and attack the animals or whatever. Unleashing your dreams is like releasing them. Don't hold onto it. Let it go. Give it to me. Trust that you're going to trust the process and believe in it. I love it because, a lot of times, we hold onto our dreams. A lot of times, we don't even believe in our dreams. We don't even believe that we're allowed to dream. A lot of times, we look at little kids and think how joyous they are. But I see it. Where a little kid is dressed up in a princess outfit, and she has this attitude. She's walking like a princess, and the light is coming out of that little kid. I bet we were the same way when we were kids. I can't remember when I was a baby or when I was a toddler of my dreams. All I remember is I put my little dollies out there, and I was teaching them or coaching them. But I also remember how I felt. That excitement and that's the same thing. We can have dreams. We can have a dream to have a better relationship with our loved ones or go on a vacation that we love. We can have those dreams. And that's what I'm saying, "Unleash those damn dreams." Don't hold it in, because if you do not, a dream stays a dream if you don't take action to release those dreams.

Tracey Lee: Absolutely, you're wrong every time you don't. And I mean, we think dreams are for people who have it all together. It's almost like a luxury to dream. I feel like we've adopted this mindset of putting a nose to the grindstone. Stay in your lane, work hard, and do all the things. I was that girl. Just keep working, you know, duty over dreams every single day. That was my life, and it literally eroded my soul. It was eroding me from the inside out. And that was showing up on the outside. It was brutal. I felt the need for change in my life physically, and that's when I decided, okay, I have decisions to make. I mean, that's where I was. I don't know where you were. Like, what was your moment when you were like, oh no, the F-bomb is going off in your head? You're like, something has to change. What was your defining moment, Christine?

Christina Singhal: Do you mean getting off the damn hamster wheel?

Tracey Lee: Yeah, whatever you want to call it.

Christina Singhal: I worked for a corporate company. I felt like I was a puppet because of the way that we were trapped—everything I studied, the independence, everything felt like it got stripped. It's like, damn, I literally felt I was tiptoeing to death. I'm doing what the rest of my peers were doing. You feel like you're in jail. You just mark all those things as one day closer. Today, I'm going to work because it takes me one day closer to retirement. And then when I heard one of these personal development guys, Bob Proctor, teaching, you can live to work. When I see people working when they're 86 years old, it's like, okay, so I'm in my 50s. That means I've got 30 more years of going to work every day, thinking it's one day closer to retirement. It is dumb, Tracey. And if I've got 30 years of doing something that I love doing, something that gives me joy. Here's the other thing that I realized, it's like, damn it, God gifted me with spiritual gifts and talents. Everybody has something very unique to that person. If you live into that, not only does that give you life, but you also are benefiting people around you. That's a ripple effect, correct?

Tracey Lee: Yeah, the ripple effect. Everybody wins. Nobody wins when you stay playing small. When you stop giving yourself permission to dream. Nobody wins. So if I'm a woman who's watching this summit and, you know, we're all in this together. Years ago, I was just like, go, go, go, go, go for everybody else but me. What would you say to that woman who is not even sure what that first step looks like when it comes to unleashing those dreams, at least a little bit? What do you think her first step could be, and why do we struggle so much with this, Christina? We all share the same struggles, we just have our own unique experiences attached to them.

Christina Singhal: Okay, so, first and foremost, and I'm talking from experience, I thought dreaming is for kids. Remember, I was telling the story about the little girl and the princess outfit. It's like, a lot of times, we take it that dreaming is not for adults, that dreaming is for kids. We are grown-ups now. We need to go to the grind, earn some money, go back home, and clean up. Clean up the house, do the house chores, keep everybody happy, serve everybody, go back to work, and repeat. Rinse and repeat the whole time. That's the hamster wheel. So, to answer your question as to what they can do. I think one of the first things, and that was one of my first realizations, it's that we deserve a dream. We have the right to a dream. And even if you're from a spiritual standpoint, I'm supposed to serve. I'm a regionally registered nurse also, so I'm supposed to just serve, serve, serve, until I realize, well, hold on, I'm created for more than just serving, and to be able to do the right thing, to do it with life, I need to tap into my capabilities. I think the first tip is to understand that you have the right to a dream. And I'm not talking about a dream, like going to be in Cirque du Soleil or something. I'm talking about who you are in your life. Your role in that dream. If you have that desire to have a great relationship with your spouse or with siblings or whatever, there are some dreams that you have that you want to be able to communicate easier or better with somebody. It might be you want to have a job where you don't feel that back-to-school feeling every morning when you tap into work, or you leave your soul at the door. It's like, you go in because if you spend eight, nine hours a day, do it where you love what you're doing, even if it's not a zillion amount of money, but you love what you're doing. A lot of times, we have financial means. Financially, I earned a lot of money, but I was at work doing, grinding, and not enjoying life. It's like you rob yourself of that beautiful life that you were given. Understand that you have the right to a dream.

Tracey Lee: Yeah, I think the feeling of worthiness is key. Our worthiness, our level of self-worth, is what either keeps us from even dreaming or keeps us listening to all the other people around us. They become our compass because we're so vulnerable. We're vulnerable, not even realizing it. The awareness that you're even in this spot of, holy shit, I don't even dream. Like, I haven't thought about something that I want in years. I've been so consumed with all the giving that I do just on autopilot. What's going on in my heart? How do you connect to your heart? What do you do to get into that spot where you're like, Oh my gosh, I want to serve people like I did nursing but in a different way. How did you get into that heart spot?

Christina Singhal: Well, first and foremost, I've listened to people, so I learned to listen very, very well. Not only listening to people, but I listened to people's dreams, and I just wanted to quickly go back to something. A dream can be anything: a vision, a goal. You can call it whatever it is, but that's what you're going after, and I know when I saw my patients, freedom from their physical ailments was the dream. This got me thinking, I'm going to one day have somebody come in, excuse me for this, change my diaper, and I'm going to be freaking miserable because I didn't risk anything. I realized I'm in my 50s, and if God grants me, I'm going to be in my 80s or 90s. By golly, the day I lay my head down, I want to be tired of being busy with things that I love. I want it to know I did everything I wanted to do. Even if I didn't reach that goal, I took action, step after step after step, and the journey was freaking amazing. Success is the journey toward that goal, that dream, that vision.

Tracey Lee: Yes, that's what success is. It's the journey of moving toward something that allows us to be greater in our true selves, right?

Christina Singhal: Right.

Tracey Lee: Amazing, oh my gosh, I love, love, love it. I love it so much. And you know, you said a couple of things that really resonated with me. The mention of risk. Not risking anything. I think that is key. We need to understand there is a risk. There is a sacrifice, you know, like, it might be money, it might be time, it might be leaving behind something that you've been a part of for years. It might be giving up what you have for something you want, and that's what you did right.

Christina Singhal: The big thing, Tracey, was to find the doubters. Remember when I was saying that I was so busy listening to others? I felt I needed his approval for everything in my life that I wanted to do. It's like, when I talk to my family, and they ask, "How are you going to do that kind of thing?" And then I realized, and I think that was one of the awareness that I had to understand, they do the best they can do, but you can't, for the life of you, rely on their opinions to choose what's right for you. It starts here, we are created as amazing individuals with amazing power. You have to be your biggest fan. Not in a selfish way, but in an uplifting way. And that's one of the things I've been doing. I have positive affirmation. I'll stand and say, come on, get it together. I had to do it yesterday.

Tracey Lee: What about the Wonder Woman pose? Hands on the hips and stand in the Wonder Woman pose in the shower. You will feel like you can take on anything. It's like, oh yeah, bring it on. It's so good, you know? And I think when it comes to doubters, they're not there to serve you. They're there to serve themselves, and they don't mean that in a negative, intentional way. At least for some people, maybe. It can be disturbing for them because what you're doing or what you're dreaming of stepping into is beyond their scope of seeing you in that position, in that way, so they don't want you to leave the way they've always seen you.

Christina Singhal: They don't want you rocking their world because you are messing with the status quo. You want to have a powerful, supportive, and strong inner voice because you are going to mess up with your status quo. But damn it, then there is that freedom and that ability on the other side when you realize as you step over this terror barrier.

Tracey Lee: Yeah, exactly. And that's why you have to experience these things. And it means you have to take the risks, and you have to take a chance on yourself. It's the only way you're going to experience it. And, you know, step into it with the right attitude, right? When I spoke in the beginning if you have an attitude that you're not going to be able to do it. Well, you're not going to be able to do it. It's a mind game we're always playing. We're going against the grain of what we believed our whole lives. When I was reading about the meaning of defy, which means to refuse to obey. Like, hello. Think about that for a minute. Refuse to obey. Do you want to obey the people who don't see your worthiness of achieving and going after your dreams?

Christina Singhal: That's that puppet on a string. Then, you play the role of the puppet on a string.

Tracey Lee: What was your story about doubters? What's your story?

Christina Singhal: So, really, it started four years ago when I was working for a corporate company. I struggled because it was cultural. We've got cultural differences between me and my tall, dark, and handsome man. It's these cultural struggles and then the way that we raise our cases and religious differences. It was just that I hit that dark crossroad when you don't know what to do. And looking back, I'm grateful for it because that was pushing me, that corner push was getting me out of my own damn way, getting out of myself. Because one of two things, either you're going to disintegrate when you hit that crossroad in your life, that dark crossroad. I mean, everything that I feared, that fear that I'm going to feel. I feared divorce and depression. Either I'm going to go further down that dark bit in my life, disintegrate, or I need to seek help. And I did. I'm grateful for my faith, and then faith brought me into personal development. I didn't even know what personal development was at that time, or mindset change. And that is where things change. And I'm so grateful I got into it because learning and understanding the power that we have in ourselves was how I gained confidence in my own life. And with that confidence, that dream that I wanted, that wish that I had, that goal that I had to have a great relationship with my partner with vibration matching up with it. And for that, I'm super, super grateful. I've made changes in my life. It's these things that I really have been dreaming and wishing for. Applying what I've been teaching as a coach because I've been a student first before, I became a coach, and applying that has given me so much confidence and so much knowledge to the point that I'm like a steamroller. Sometimes I feel like a steamroller. There's no turning back. I can do it. I know anybody else can do this.

Tracey Lee: It's a lot of discipline. You have to be very disciplined. We have to parent ourselves. I mean, that's what my experience is anyway. You've got to go back and parent yourself. So you stay on, and you stay focused because we lose focus easily. We let those doubters in. Especially if we're having that vulnerable moment, we allow those doubtful, you know, ideas from others, or even ourselves, because we're our worst inner critic, to penetrate. And those things can attack our dreams. So you carry a really beautiful message on your phone. I remember you sharing. I want you to share, what is the story behind that message? And why is it so important to you?

Christina Singhal: I don't know if they can see it. Yeah, don't tell people your dreams, show them. That's the message I have. I saw this quote and it's like, I needed to say that based on a conversation I had with my daughter a couple of years ago. We were heading to the mountains and going on a hike with the cousins. And I was mentioning to us, I wonder if your mom is going to have a house in the mountains, it's going to be at the lake. and she's like, "Okay, mom." I said, "Do you believe me?" and she said, "Mom, I believe you because you believe it." I briefly felt good, and then I didn't feel good because I suddenly put myself on the spot. I felt guilty because what if I'm not producing this house, what if I'm not going to be doing what I told my kids? I'm going to disappoint my kids. This mom who is all about life and dreams and going for things is not producing, not showing. So I didn't feel good. And then when I saw this quote, I saved it on my phone. You need to protect your dreams like a newborn baby. You need to nurture it with love and patience. You need to guard it against naysayers and questions and anything that can threaten that baby, that dream. And also you need to step up, and you're going to have times when you're guarding it. Also, sometimes there is going to be something that's going to challenge that dream, and you need to know that it's okay. You need to just keep going and move forward. So for me, that's important because I realized also, that it's one thing you have accountable partners, fellow dream builders. For me, fellow dream builders are like-minded people and who you share your dreams with. The rest, you show them and walk the talk.

Tracey Lee: Yes, walk the talk, baby. Yeah, you have to and you know we can't tend to the fire on our own all the time. We do need other people to help us tend to our fire, and that is why having the right people in your corner is so important.

Christina Singhal: Like, I'm not in this alone. You cannot do it alone. Surround yourself with people who support you, people who understand, and people who have dreams. It's not your dream. They have their own dream, but you guys keep it in your circle of trust and support. I have mastermind groups. We do mastermind groups, me, you, mainstream. My God, just like the course. It's like writing an ebook, things that I said I'm never going to do, look at it. I've got an ebook, girls. Yeah, it's all there. It's amazing.

Tracey Lee: You are a powerful, powerful soul. You are helping so many women. You walk the talk, Christina. You're a force. You don't just think about it. You take action. You're an action woman, and you lead with your heart. I just adore you.

Christina Singhal: Thank you, Tracey.

To watch Tracey Lee's interview with Christina Singhal, scan the QR Code below.

Margaret Dennis

Founder and CEO of EVOLV coaching

https://www.linkedin.com/in/margaretdennis/
https://www.facebook.com/evolvcoaching
https://www.instagram.com/evolvcoaching/
https://evolvcoaching.com/
https://www.unshakeable-me.com/

Margaret is a Women's Life Empowerment & Grief Coach, TEDx Speaker, #1 International Bestselling Author, Certified Dare2Declare™ Vision Board Facilitator, Founder & CEO of EVOLV coaching, and Co-Founder of Unshakeable ME Inc. Summer Camps for Teenage Girls.

In 2008, Margaret faced the unbearable loss of her 3-day-old son, twin to her daughter, Lily. This devastating experience plunged her into the depths of grief, where she confronted her deepest fears and unearthed layers of past trauma. Within her pain, she discovered an unshakeable inner strength that ignited her life's purpose: to empower women who have experienced trauma and grief to feel so worthy that they can't help but live a life of joy and passion.

Today, Margaret feeds her passion by supporting women to heal and find joy through her exclusive 1:1 coaching program, her Sacred Oasis membership program, customized workshops, motivational writing, leading at women's healing retreats, and keynote speaking.

Becoming Unshakeable: A Journey From Fear to Empowerment

By Margaret Dennis

TRACEY & JENN MOMENTS

Jenn Iannuzzi: Just kidding. I'm not muted.

Tracey Lee: Oh my gosh. We need these bloopers. If people only knew what's going on behind the scenes. All fun things happen behind the scenes in the chat. It's like, yeah, go, give me this, give me that. This is the stuff that makes all of this just mesh and work, right? We're building this like cool energy behind the scenes. It's so fun.

Jenn Iannuzzi: Archer, who's one of our producers for the show here. He just wrote in the chat, "You scared me," because I've made this mistake like three times already. That was for you, Archer.

Tracey Lee: I want to do a shoutout right now, actually, and I'm going to do multiple of these, but I had to make a very big decision very close to this event happening because I didn't realize that I was the one who would have to make all of this actually look like it does. And I'm like, pardon? Okay, there are some things you need to know. You can get out of your damn way as long as it's something that lights you up, and that stuff I thought I had to do. All this behind the scenes stuff would have dropped my vibe and created stress. So, I couldn't show up for everyone this way. I had the blessing to connect with this amazing company called PodPlant, and Mike and Archer are in the background. You don't see them. Oh, I love you, and they are freaking awesome. They're giving us the confidence to do what we're doing here. They're making it fun for us. We feel held. We feel supported. And I just want to shout out to PodPlant. They will rock your friggin podcast or whatever you want to do. They're the broadcasting people that have, I think, 35-plus years in the business. PodPlant. Look them up, and we're going to drop links in here so you guys can know who they are.

Jenn Iannuzzi: I didn't let anyone forget them.

Tracey Lee: Well, how are we doing? Jenn, I'm making people cry now.

Jenn Iannuzzi: I know, well, this is the usual. If you spend long enough with Tracey, she just pores into your soul and eventually, you're going to start crying. So it was bound to happen. It will happen again.

Tracey Lee: These sessions are powerful. I'm just, wow. And I know we're headed in for two more powerhouse women. And this woman, she and I connected on a deep level because she has a love for children and for helping girls, too. And I know that she and I are going to do something big one day when it comes to the girl's camp I want to create. She's already rocking out supporting girls with summertime programs in camps, like, thank God, he just knows how to bring the right people together, right?

Jenn Iannuzzi: Let's introduce Margaret.

Tracey Lee: Do it. Do it.

Introduction

Meet Margaret Demis, the powerhouse CEO of Evolve Coaching and co-founder of Unshakable Me Summer Camps for Teenage Girls. Margaret is the guiding light behind "Becoming Unshakable," a transformative journey from fear to empowerment. Her story is one of incredible resilience; she turned her grief into a global mission to help women rediscover joy and become unshakable. As a TEDx speaker and educator, Margaret has transformed her adversities into a call to action, leading others from a place of loss to profound strength and resilience.

Margaret's life is filled with bold choices and a deep passion for growth. If she could afford any car, she'd be behind the wheel of a Lamborghini—reflecting her fearless approach to life. She's the type to cannonball into a pool rather than dip a toe in first, embodying the boldness that defines her work and personal journey.

Growing up in Acton, Ontario, Margaret now resides in Ottawa, where she continues to lead and inspire. Her favorite pastime is traveling, which feeds her love for exploration and learning. Science was her favorite subject in school, hinting at her curious and analytical mind.

Margaret's personal favorites speak to her refined yet adventurous spirit. She adores anything chocolate when it comes to dessert, and her favorite breakfast is classic eggs and bacon. If she ever had to change her first name, she'd go for Catherine with a 'K'—a name that carries a sense of elegance and strength.

When it comes to learning, Margaret is a doer. She prefers to learn by doing, embracing the hands-on experiences that life throws her way. She's a book-smart woman who values knowledge, yet she's never afraid to make bold decisions, a trait that's evident in her personal and professional life.

Margaret's hero is her grandmother, a woman who likely instilled in her the values of strength and resilience. Her eyes are her favorite body part, perhaps because they reflect the wisdom and determination she's gained over the years. She loves quoting *Pretty Woman*, a movie that, much like her, tells a story of transformation and empowerment.

Her favorite word in another language is "Je t'aime," which speaks to her loving and compassionate nature. And when asked what makes her hopeful, Margaret's answer is simple yet profound: her daughter. It's this love for her daughter that fuels her drive to create a better world for women, one where they can be unshakable, just like her.

INTERVIEW

Margaret Dennis: Hello!

Tracey Lee: Good, how friggin' awesome is this day?

Margaret Dennis: It's incredible. It seems like we just started it yesterday, but it's gone by really fast.

Tracey Lee: I know, we've been talking about this for four months now. And you were one of the first people to be a 'hell yes' when we started.

Margaret Dennis: Oh yeah, oh yeah. There was no question. I just fell in love with the name of the summit. So, I was like, yep, must do it.

Tracey Lee: Right? Oh my God. So, so right. And let's just go there for a minute. Let's talk about your biggest get-out-of-our-damn-way moment that's helped you catapult to all of these amazing things you create even better and more. Let's talk about that.

Margaret Dennis: Sure. For me, this is my 'yes' year. I'm saying yes to everything. And I'm leaning into my intuition. What does it feel good to do? I did some coaching with my fellow coaches a while back and I was like, hey, I'm getting involved in a whole bunch of things, but I need to be able to figure out what another speaker talked about before. Does it align with your values? You know, what are you doing? Make sure that you're doing the things that really light you up. And my number one thing for anything that I choose to do is it has to be fun. If I don't enjoy it, I won't do it. I won't put passion or time into it. I'll drag my feet up across to me.

And for me, speaking on a stage is the ultimate fun. I love speaking. Anyone who's known me ever in my life, knows that I love to talk. And I'm sure a lot of them are giggling right now. But I do, I enjoy sharing knowledge, sharing information, and being out there. And so when this came up, not only did I love the name of it, but I loved what you stood for. And I love the fact that we connected on the teen girl level, that there was a lot of alignment with what we were doing. So, for me, it was a 'hell yes' right from the beginning.

Tracey Lee: That's amazing. That's so good. So, so beautiful. I love all that. And, you know, you work with people, and I love what you do. It's big stuff, helping people move through grief and creating resilience through that experience. How does that even work? I would say the last big thing I experienced, well, we lost our dog just about a month ago now. That was big, but before that was my best friend to cancer. How do you move through grief and create resilience?

Margaret Dennis: I think the biggest thing you can do when you're moving through grief is connection. Connection with other people, connection with your family, and connection with your loved ones. So often, when we're in our grief, we retreat. We go into ourselves. We hibernate. We don't reach out for help. Usually, because we don't know what we need, which is very normal. Our grief brain kicks in, we think we just have to get through the next hour, the next day. And it depends on the type of grief, too, because there are so many different types of grief, which a lot of people are unaware of. With grief, it's a journey. It's something that, when you've experienced grief, it lives with you forever. It is never something that you get over. It isn't ever something that you know you can just put a band-aid over it and hope it'll go away.

A lot of the way our North American society teaches us is like here you go, you get three days, go grieve and then we want you back in the office. And everyone around you wants you to go back to being the same person that you were before, but you're not because grief changes you. So, for someone who's going through grief, a lot of the time, they feel alone. And then you have all the people around you who are trying to be so supportive. And they really, God love them, they are. But we don't teach people how to support those in grief, either. We say all the wrong things. We'll say things to someone who's grieving like, "Oh, you're so brave. You're going to get through this. Be strong." But what they don't realize is they're saying that for them. They're not saying it for the person who's grieving because I'll tell you, for me, when I've been in the depths of grief, the last thing I wanted to do was be brave or strong. I just wanted to go find a corner, curl up, cry, and just have somebody take care of me. But that wasn't possible when things happened to me. You have these societal expectations that you still have to, you know, chin up, buddy, just keep going. When we find people who are still grieving three, four, five, six months later, a year later, or decades later, we don't, as a society, know how to help people.

So what I do in my practice with the women that I coach who've been through trauma and grief is we get in touch with the feelings that have been buried for so long. If you don't acknowledge how you feel, allow yourself the time, and permit yourself to feel what you're feeling, it's just going to keep building up inside your body. Your body holds on to every experience and every emotion that you have ever had. And so over time, all these little grief events and some of the big catastrophic ones, if you're not expressing them and releasing these emotions, they just build up like a pressure cooker. You find when you get into your 40s, 50s, and 60s, you're suffering from depression and anxiety, can't sleep, and even have trouble making decisions. All these things start creeping up and you're wondering where it's coming from. A really big contributing factor could be grief. So what I do in the sessions with the women that I work with is really dive into giving them permission to feel, giving them a safe space to be vulnerable, permitting them to feel whatever they feel because a lot of the time, we judge ourselves on how we feel. Say we were with someone who had gone through a long bout of cancer and then passed away, they could actually feel a sense of relief and then feel shame and guilt around that exactly because you definitely wouldn't turn to someone and say, "Oh my god, I'm so relieved, you know, their suffering is over." But it's a relief for both of you, it's not just who's passed away, it's you as well. We aren't allowed to say that, and so we keep it to ourselves, and we shame ourselves for feeling the feelings that we have. There's so much more that comes up in grief than just sadness. There's anger, resentment, shame, guilt, relief, you name it; it's in there. And so by working on actually releasing those, you give space for people to start to feel something other than sadness, other than anger. It feels lighter. It opens up the door for people to bring some more joy into their lives. And we work on the fact that it's okay to feel joy because that's a really big factor, too. Somebody loses a spouse, a child, or a parent. Sometimes, we feel like we don't deserve to be happy because they're gone. And even then, we push down the joy. We push down the idea of being happy. Again, out of guilt. That's not the way it's supposed to be. We are here, we are put on this earth to be happy. And things are going to happen but how we deal with them is so important.

Tracey Lee: Wow. So powerful. And I think when we're going through any kind of grief, we want to create distractions for ourselves, not to think about it. And that isn't going to serve you in the long run because that's unexpressed emotions. And then it just gets stored in your body. They say the last place that disease shows up is actually in the body. I'm sure you've seen that with a lot of your clients, physical symptoms come a lot of times from grief. I think you said something really important, too, and I'm curious how we support someone going through grief because we aren't coached either. How do we do that?

Margaret Dennis: Supporting someone with grief ultimately comes down to actually being there for them. And when you say to someone, "I'm so sorry for your loss," leave it at that. Don't say to someone, "I know exactly how you feel." Because you don't, you absolutely don't. Grief is a very unique experience. We may both have experienced the loss of a spouse, but how I dealt with it and how you deal with it would be very different because we have all these different memories and experiences that come along with that. So, if you want to support someone in grief effectively, be there for them. Being there without judgment is a really big one. Don't judge how they feel. Don't judge how they're expressing their grief. Let them grieve in a way that is what they need to do. And when you say you're going to be there, be there, show up at their house, make sure they're not still in their pajamas from two weeks ago, that they've had a shower, and bring them some food.

So often, what happens, especially when we lose someone, is we're in survival mode for the first few days: we plan the funeral, we go to the funeral, we make it through. When people say, "I just feel like I walked through a day," your grief brain was keeping you on acting just to survive those days. And then a couple of weeks go by, and you're now relaxed to really feel the grief, but everybody else around you is moved on. And so, again, you're alone. Being with somebody and allowing them to just, you know, if they want to cry, let them cry. If they want to just sit there with you and not say anything, let them do that, too. One of the biggest things is if they'll let you give them a hug, and if you can, hug. A friend of mine, Risa, teaches about healthy touch, and I learned this summer that if you hug for 30 seconds, that's when growth starts to happen. That's when healing starts to happen because you start to release all these oxytocin and the good hormones in your body, and people need that connection. A hug is an amazing way to connect with someone. So, if they will let you, you need to ask permission because a lot of people retreat, they're afraid that if they hug, they will lose their emotions. They will start to cry, and then they won't stop. I will tell you that you will; you may end up falling asleep while you're crying, but you will stop. You know, when toddlers cry, they cry really, really, really hard, and then at the end, they gasp for air. You will do that, too. So, when someone's going through grief, just allow them to be who they need to be in that moment and let them express whatever they are feeling without judgment. That's the biggest part. Don't judge somebody how they grieve or how they move on. Yeah, that's another big part. We judge how people move on.

Tracey Lee: It's really, really powerful. Oh, my goodness. I'm so happy. I know we spoke about this because everyone has someone they know, or maybe they're experiencing it themselves. I think this kind of information allows us to reflect upon ourselves. And how we're showing up. And also just go introspective and ask ourselves, why am I so uncomfortable? Why do I want to approach it this way? And so much opportunity to learn and grow within any kind of experience like that, right? That can be looked upon as something that's just so tragic, but there is beauty in everything. There is beauty in everything.

Margaret Dennis: I think biologically, we're wired to run away from grief because we see it as a threat. We see someone grieving, and we're like, "Oh no, I can't have that touch me." So you back away, right? Our fight or flight kicks in. And we're like, "Oh." So that's why we say to people, "Be brave, be strong." Because if I tell you to be brave and strong, and you are, it means the grief can't touch me. A lot of the time, we move away from people without even realizing we're moving away. It can be a very unconscious move, but it's our fight-or-flight response that kicks in.

Tracey Lee: What got you to do this? What happened? What's your story? How did you become someone? I know we're going to go into the Unshakable Me and all that, which is so beautiful. And I never know how these conversations are going to go because I just really follow my intuition. I think you know we're both being guided together, which is why it's so beautiful, but can you share what is the story that brought you to do this in the first place, Margaret?

Margaret Dennis: Well, it started about 15 years ago. I was pregnant with twins. We'd had six years of infertility, so these twins were a gift for us. I ended up going into labor really early, at five and a half months, and had the twins. I had a boy and a girl. Our son was very, very sick, and he passed away three days after the twins were born. His name was Isaac. My daughter Lily was the strong one, she survived, and she is just the most incredible kid. So, I'm a new mom, I have a child who's passed away and a child who has survived, who's in the neonatal intensive care unit, struggling to survive herself. And so you'll have to make a choice. I can love my daughter, or I can grieve for my son. It came down to I'm going to love my daughter right now because she needs me. And I just buried the grief because I'm like, I can't deal with this right now. If I gave in to the grief, I thought I wouldn't be able to be the mom I needed to be.

Our daughter was in the hospital for six and a half months. We finally brought her home the size of a newborn. She was about five-and-a-half pounds when we brought her home on oxygen and tube feeding. There was a lot of support that she needed. Her life for the first four years was a lot of hospital visits. I dove into that. But I never lied to her about her brother. I thought she's a twin. They have a connection. And so I was talking to her about Isaac while I was feeding her when she was an infant. She grew up knowing about him. As she got older and really understood that he had died, her grieving process started. It was under, you know, answering her questions, crying with her, talking about where he went and what he was doing.

We started doing that. And I thought, great, I can talk about him now. I still cry; things on the radio make me cry, but I'm okay. I think I've grieved. I'm good. I'm moving on. And then, in 2021, I had the opportunity to do a TED Talk. And I had always wanted to tell the story about what had happened because I thought it could help somebody else. And so I started writing my TED Talk. As I was writing it, the tears just started to come. I realized I hadn't dealt with my grief very well at all because I could not write or say my speech without breaking down. I thought I was never going to be able to give my speech. Like, how am I going to do this? This is like my bucket list moment. I need to be able to do this. So, I worked with my cousin who does EFT, and she helped me sort of just get some things in place so that I could do my speech. But I wrote about my daughter's experience in grief and why she, as a child, knew how to grieve better than we do as adults, right? When she was sad, she cried. When she had questions, she asked about them. And when people asked her if she had siblings, she was very honest and said, "I had a brother, but he died." And so she used the grief as a way her life was. I watched how she integrated that into her life and became an extremely strong young girl. I thought we, as adults, suck at how we deal with our grief. We don't allow our people as adults to grieve.

When I did my speech, I talked about the difference between telling people that you're sad versus telling people that you're stressed. If someone came into your office and said, "Oh my God, I'm so stressed," you'd be like, "Oh man, me too." Like, it's just a horrible workload. Right? We give people this badge of honor. Like, oh, I thought you were stressed, but if I walked into your office and you said, "Hey, Margaret, how are you doing?" And I said, "Tracey, you know what? I'm so sad today because I'm really missing my son." Blank headlights, you'd be like deer back and up. People don't know how to deal with that. When I did my speech and did a lot of research into grief and how we deal with it, it put a fire in my belly. I'm like, I am not the only person out here in this world who has experienced the fact that I haven't dealt with grief. And I had a lot of support around me. Don't get me wrong. I had a beautiful family and friends who were very, very supportive of everything that we went through. But I wanted to get out into the world, start educating people, and let them know there's a different way of doing this, and we need to support people better.

I started with doing workshops and educating. I'll be honest: I did hesitate to go into coaching, not coaching in general, but coaching women going through grief because I thought I was a very empathic person. I take on everybody's emotions. I have learned not to, but I thought if I do this, it's going to be too heavy for me and I couldn't be the coach I needed to be for them. But the exact opposite happened. When I started coaching women through their grief, it was incredible to watch their metamorphosis when they finally had someone to listen to them, someone that they could share their deepest emotions with, and someone that they could cry with and be 100%-raw honest. After working with them for three months, they were a completely different person. They would come to the sessions with a twinkle in their eye and a smile, and they would say, "You know what I did today? I smiled for the first time." You see the progress and it is so incredibly rewarding to be able to be that person for them. So that was my journey to get me to where I am today.

Tracey Lee: Wow. What an incredible journey you just shared. You could never have even known when that experience happened with your twins that you would have been led in the direction you are in now.

Margaret Dennis: No.

Tracey Lee: I think we need to appreciate that on a very deep level because we just have this desire to control everything that's going to happen. Let that go because it's not available to you. Control isn't even available to you. It exists in your brain, and it's screwing with you. So, you've got to just let that go and let in, right? And by letting in you trust yourself that you know you can ask. I love what you said. You said when your daughter cried. A question she asks is the things that are so simple that are so transformative, and are things that can stick. It's just amazing, you know, like, oh my gosh, this is so so beautiful. I think that grief is a life skill that we need to learn.

Margaret Dennis: We do. We really, really do, and we need to teach people.

Tracey Lee: We need to learn.

Margaret Dennis: We're all going to go through it. Grief is not, you know, selective. It's like every single person on the planet is going to experience grief in one way, shape, or form. Maybe it's that you failed your driver's test and maybe it's that you lost your house to a fire. Maybe it's your spouse who dies. There are so many different forms of grief that are on a continuum. But one thing I always, always tell my clients is what you're going through is your 100%. And what I go through is my 100%. I think a lot of us when we're in grief, if it's not your typical grief like I lost the promotion or I didn't get to go on the trip that I wanted, there's always those little bits of grief that come along. You have a neighbor whose dog died or who lost a child, you'll be like, well, you know, I'm sad, but it's not as bad as them. And then you discount your own grief, you discount your own feelings, and that's when they get pushed down. Instead of saying, you know what, they're experiencing their 100%. And this is my 100%. And giving yourself permission to feel what you feel in that moment.

I know I did it when I was in the hospital with my daughter. I would look around, and I'm like, wow, she is super stable. She's doing great. And I would because there were other kids in the hospital who weren't doing as well as she was. And when another child died in the unit, I was like, oh, I'm so grateful for my daughter. And I would feel like I couldn't be as sad about what was happening to me because they had lost their only child, I'd only lost one. You start putting yourself on this comparison. Part of it is survival in the grief. But the other part is discounting the feelings because it's scary to feel them. It's really scary to feel them because you do feel like they are so much more powerful than you.

Tracey Lee: You know what's crazy hearing you say all this? I mean, I've had so many losses in my life. I lost both my parents when I was very young, and I remember meeting with a grief counselor. She's like, you've never even processed any of this, and she was right. I hadn't. I still know there's lots of work to do. We are set up to compare ourselves with other people like, well, you know, it could be a lot worse. Lucky. It could be way worse, like other people have it way worse than you. So buckle up, suck it up, and move on. And I literally used to say that to myself. I think I used to say that to other people. And now I'm sitting here talking about this and just like, whoa. And this is what awareness does. Awareness gives us something that we can take that is tactical and bring into our own lives, and make it tangible. And tangible is really us taking an idea and bringing it into something that we can execute in a way that has an impact on our lives, and we'll deliver a different result in some way and that is really, really powerful. I was just like, drop the mic moments happening today, people. Wow. Okay. I want to talk about this whole unshakable conversation.

I feel like this has been weaving in and out of this conversation. Building that unstoppable attitude is really important, and it all works together if we're shaken, right? There were good things, good reasons why we get shaken because it's a chance to see where we have work to do. But the more we can create that unshakable foundation, the better we can handle things like grief, things like all these different things from a place of gratitude and peace and love and all of that. So, let's talk about Unshakable Me. What is that all about?

Margaret Dennis: Well, it happened this year. It was a brainchild I had, and then a colleague of mine jumped on board really quickly, too. So, between the two of us, we've created this unshakable movement, I guess you want to say. What it stemmed from is that women that I work with, a lot of the time when we're processing the emotions so that we can then start moving forward, we go back and we do some emotional transcendence work, and we go back to like, where is that emotion coming from?

A lot of the time, the 'aha' moments were like, oh, my childhood. Oh, when I was a teenager. And I started thinking like, I teach at a women's retreat, and we do all kinds of emotional work. It's amazing. The soulful camp. Highly recommended. Heather and Jenny are incredible. And I thought, what if we took their kind of idea of working on the emotional side and applied it to teenage girls because you could not pay me enough to go back to being a teenage girl. No way. Hell no. And it's a really challenging time for our girls. And guys, too, not discounting the boys, but I work with the girls. When you think about being a girl, Tracey, I'm sure you can attest to this, and every other woman on this summit can. We are controlled by our hormones, we are controlled by our emotions. We are emotional beings. And when we hit puberty and get into our teenage years, we're crazy. Within five minutes, we can go from anger to sadness to starving to laughing. And people look at you, and they're like, oh my God, where did you come from, and who are you now? Right, like you're multiple personalities within a minute.

And so what my colleague Leah and I wanted to do was to create a camp for teenage girls to come to, and we called it Unshakable Me, where they could come and learn how to make friends with their emotions, how to create learning tools that will support them now and as they move forward. But most importantly, to teach them to look within for validation about who they are because we know growing up our friendship groups and the people around us are it. And if people don't like me, they say something mean, or they bully me. It's devastating, and I think there's something wrong with me, and my self-esteem, self-confidence, and self-worth go into the toilet. That's how it works. As much as we have amazing parental support, a lot of us do, the parents are great, but they're not our peers. And so when we're in school all the time, and we're in it with our friends, and we're not being treated well, or we get told, oh my God, you're so clumsy. And sometimes it's from family, you know, you're clumsy, don't be so loud.

Tracey Lee: You're such a good girl, you're so sweet, you're so funny, you're so this, thinking it's like not a big deal, but those labels stick.

Margaret Dennis: They do, they do. And what happens is we create our identity from it and then we start to think that something's wrong with us because people are telling us negative things about ourselves. So, a big focus of the camp is to teach the girls that they're unique and amazing just because they're here. And they are teaching them how to identify their emotions. We have an emotion wheel that we give them that's got like hundreds of emotions on it. And it's like, okay, if you're sad, look on the emotion wheel. What other word in there describes how you're feeling? Are you disappointed? Are you frustrated? What's underneath that? If we can teach our girls to identify their emotions, then they can actually express them. And they can learn how to deal with them more effectively and in the process, learn that they're a good person, and believe that they're a good person. So we have amazing guest facilitators come in that help work with the girls as well. And Leah and I do a lot. We focus on play and fun and connecting to the inner child. So, we do the Unshakable Me camps and we did two this year that were just amazing. We had so much support from the community. And we're looking at doing four or more next year. Really, really excited about it. On top of that, though, we've also created Unshakable Us.

Unshakable Us is for mothers and daughters. It's to help them heal communication or build communication and connection. Sometimes, it's our moms, right? When we're daughters, we look up to our moms. And our moms may not have had the best childhood either. So how do we help them heal so they can work with their daughters, too? It's a lot of building that connection and support and teaching them that we're all human.

Tracey Lee: Oh my goodness, amazing. Wow, it's really beautiful. I connect with everything, obviously, that you're saying on a very soulful level. We aren't being supported at a young age the way we need to be supported. And again, it's not because of our parents. It's not because maybe you don't have parents and their influence in your life. Whatever it is, everyone's doing the best they can. And when we come together as women who've had the experiences, who have the desire, and who know that this is a space that is really needed and the impact is going to be so huge for what's to come for these girls and how it impacts the ripple effect of the world. My vision for a camp is massively driven because of my childhood experiences and I didn't have a mom growing up. I want to bring moms who didn't have daughters or couldn't have daughters and bring them together. Start to create beautiful opportunities for women and girls to share love, learn how to love, and learn about themselves in a different part of themselves. I think you know everything we do, it's just about learning more about who we really are.

Margaret Dennis: It really is, and I think it can be really scary to dig into who we are, especially if we really have a poor self-image and self-esteem, like "Why would I bother? I'm not worth looking into," right? There's that. And then a lot of people start at that place, and it is 100% worth it because underneath all of it, underneath all the things that you've told yourself and all the things you've let yourself believe, you are an incredible person with so much to offer the world. You are unique in and of yourself, and the world needs you. The world needs you to be you. There's no one else on the planet like you, so it is worth doing the work to let that crap go and step into your power and be that woman that you were meant to be or be that girl you truly are.

Tracey Lee: Absolutely, absolutely, and you know, every day can be your new day. And even if you're on the road to something great, make every day your new day because it puts you in a beginner's mindset as well. I think that's really important too. I mean, it's important for me, even as a coach, because I want to meet everyone where they are. And if you're a woman right now watching this, and you're looking for support when it comes to grief, I hope you've been taking notes because I think when you're going through it, or you're supporting, or you just know, eventually, you will be experiencing it. These are life skills. If you're just out of a crossroads, you're like, I don't know, I just know life has to be better than it is right now, or I know that there's something I'm supposed to do that isn't what I'm doing right now, you're not alone and today can be your day one. And I think it comes back to asking, expressing your emotions, and knowing that that's actually part of stepping into your power, stepping into empowerment. You have to be able to do that. And do it in silence if you need to. Just do it. Wherever you can feel comfortable right now, just do it.

Margaret Dennis: We're so afraid to try to express our emotions, but it is empowering. When you release them, they don't control you anymore. They'll still come up. Don't get me wrong, it's not like one cry and you're done. But as you allow those emotions to come up, you step into your power. And when they come up again, you're like, okay, I can handle this. This is good.

Tracey Lee: Yes, absolutely. Amazing. Thank you, thank you, thank you. I know you're not feeling great today, but you showed up and were smiling. I'm so grateful for you. And I just love, love, love the synergies we have together, becoming unshakable, a journey from fear to empowerment. You rock this; you're amazing. And I just can't wait to hear more about what's to come for you. So thank you from the bottom of my heart.

Margaret Dennis: Thank you, Tracey, for having me. And thank you for putting this on. This has been an incredible opportunity and an incredible event. So thank you very much.

Tracey Lee: You're so welcome. Thank you.

To watch Tracey Lee's interview with Margaret Dennis, scan the QR Code below.

Nubbia Quezada

https://www.instagram.com/nubbiaquezada
https://www.nubbiaquezada.com/

Nubbia Quezada embarked on a deep spiritual awakening that ignited her transformative journey and a profound connection with the spiritual realm. Following the heart-wrenching loss of her brother to the grips of mental illness, her journey led her to the core of her being - revealing the authentic woman that lived within her all along.

As she crossed the path of self-discovery, she felt an irresistible urge to share her story—a tale of resilience and renewal—that resonated deeply with many souls. Through this connection, she found her purpose: Guiding others to embrace their higher selves through the power of healing and embracing their truth.

Nubbia is a mother of three remarkable children, who are her grounding force. Her journey has taught her the power of unlocking her inner potential and embracing life with abundance, gratitude, and boundless love. She stands as a beacon of hope, a testament to the strength of the human spirit, and a guide for those seeking to illuminate their own paths. With unwavering dedication, Nubbia strives to inspire and empower, creating a world where each heart finds its rhythm, and each soul finds its truth.

Awakened Healing:
7 Steps to a Renewed Life

By Nubbia Quezada

TRACEY & JENN MOMENTS

Jenn Iannuzzi: What a legacy Nubbia is going to leave.

Tracey Lee: Can we just give a round of applause for our speakers?

Tracey Lee: Oh my gosh, this has been—I just looked at how long we've been on—a seven-hour day.

Jenn Iannuzzi: We have two more days left of this.

Tracey Lee: Wow.

Jenn Iannuzzi: Can I absorb that much?

Tracey Lee: I just did some push-ups. I think you and I need to have some kind of a contest going about what we're doing to keep our energy up throughout the day. Let's challenge each other on the break to do something to keep our energy up.

Jenn Iannuzzi: Okay, I'm in.

Tracey Lee: You're in?

Jenn Iannuzzi: Usually, you'd be proud of me. I'm drinking a lot of water today, so much water.

Tracey Lee: I'm proud of you. And you know what? We'll challenge each other. We're going to challenge all the other people too. We're going to challenge everybody to keep their energy up.

Jenn Iannuzzi: Oh, it's so fun. We could have little activities and little challenges. Let's come up with some ideas tonight, Tracey. Let's jot down some ideas.

Tracey Lee: And one other thing, how are we liking this music? Like, does everyone love this theme song?

Jenn Iannuzzi: Everyone loves the theme song, Tracey.

Tracey Lee: It's freaking awesome.

Jenn Iannuzzi: We love the theme song.

Tracey Lee: So good. Okay, we have one more. You know, one more beautiful soul rounding out this day one. Nubbia is just, well, you'll just fall in love with her because she's just like this heart-centered woman to bring us all down to a calm place. Okay, so just feel that your heart gets comfy. And Jen, you're going to bring Nubbia in, reel her in for us all, so we can just get ready to feel her vibe.

Introduction

Meet Nubbia, the remarkable woman leading us through "Awakened Healing: Seven Steps to a Renewed Life." Her journey is nothing short of a spiritual odyssey—a word she loves because it perfectly encapsulates her path from personal tragedy to profound resilience. Nubbia's story is one of empowerment, as she now guides others to embrace their higher selves and own truths. With a heart brimming with love and unyielding dedication, she's here to inspire us all toward self-discovery and the boundless potential within each of us.

Nubbia's mornings begin at 5:30 a.m., a routine that reflects her commitment to embracing each day with purpose and energy. She's a morning person through and through, finding joy in the early hours when the world is quiet and full of promise. Her favorite type of weather is summer, a season that resonates with her warm and vibrant spirit.

Growing up in Toronto, Nubbia has always been active, with the gym being her favorite subject in school. This passion for movement continues today, as her favorite way to work out is strength training. She enjoys the challenge and the empowerment that comes from building physical strength, a metaphor for the inner strength she cultivates in herself and others.

Nubbia's hero is our Divine Creator, a source of inspiration and guidance in her life. Her spiritual beliefs are deeply rooted, and she believes in the existence of ghosts and soulmates, reflecting her connection to the unseen and the profound.

When it comes to food, Nubbia's best dish is pasta, a comforting and hearty meal that she enjoys sharing with loved ones. Her favorite Disney character is Mulan, a symbol of strength, courage, and resilience—traits that Nubbia embodies in her own life. The way to her heart? Love, pure and simple.

Nubbia has a deep curiosity about the human psyche, always seeking to understand more about the mind and soul. This interest drives her work in healing and self-discovery, where she empowers others to unlock their potential. If she could have any superpower, she'd choose to fly, symbolizing her desire for freedom and transcendence.

Her childhood fear of clowns has long been replaced by a strong, fearless spirit, and she believes that her 12-year-old self would indeed think she's cool today—a testament to how far she's come. Whether it's winning contests, enjoying a salty snack, or showering at night, Nubbia lives life with intention and gratitude.

Nubbia hopes to be remembered for the impact she's made in helping human beings. Her legacy is one of love, guidance, and the unwavering belief that we all have the power to transform our lives. Through her journey, she shows us that the path to renewal is an odyssey worth taking, and she's here to walk it with us.

INTERVIEW

Nubbia Quezada: Hey, can you hear me?

Tracey Lee: I can hear you.

Nubbia Quezada: I think I was smiling the entire time. Whatever you guys are drinking or having, I wanted to see your energy. Oh my gosh, it's amazing.

Tracey Lee: Well, I am being fueled by all of you, like, really, truly, from the very beginning, you know, having amazing Jenn, having the people behind the scenes supporting us, and then having all of you women here who I know. We're all just loving on each other. Love is a powerful energy. It's a powerful emotion, and it just makes us feel things that we can't even express. I don't even know how to express love. You just express it through, I guess, how you give and what you do and just how you show up, right?

Nubbia Quezada: Absolutely, yes, yes, I'm so happy to be here. It's been a long journey, right?

Tracey Lee: And you were one of the first people when I held this Get Out of Her Damn Way summit info call for speakers to come and just hear my vision, you were like, sign me up.

Nubbia Quezada: I was. I was super excited. I've always wanted to speak, share my message, and be someone of impact. And as soon as I heard this was an opportunity, I'm like, whether I'm prepared or not, I am jumping on it.

Tracey Lee: Yes, yes. And then we had an amazing conversation. And I think I lit a little fire under your butt. And I was just like, "Okay, Nubbia, all in, right? We need to go all in." And I know you have grown through this process. I love watching you shine. I love watching you just really step in and be that creative mover. You know that you're going to be able to have an even bigger impact because you're going to be able to give more on a grander scale. And being here a part of this is a whole part of that, right?

Nubbia Quezada: Absolutely. And I think for anyone watching is just to even see the growth and the challenges and the steps that we need to take to grow, shine, and be greater. It is a process. It's a moment when we declare that it's time and nothing is holding us back. The moment you say yes to yourself and then the rest just starts to fall into place.

Tracey Lee: And you make that your default setting as much as possible, right? Because things come at us. We have moments like we did the other day and you're like, oh, and everything was happening. Kids needed to be picked up and all the things happening at once. What do you do? Life is a bunch of peaks and valleys moments.

Nubbia Quezada: Absolutely.

Tracey Lee: For me, it's about finding that default moment, that new standard that you set for yourself to keep going back to resetting. And then you're able to step into being awake in life. You're able to receive and give. You're able to progress, move forward, forgive, and show love to yourself and other people. And so I'm so excited about our topic today. Awakened healing. Just that alone makes me feel calm and peaceful. I purposely put you at the end of our day today, because I know that you bring a softness, you bring a fierce forceness to what you do because of the impact it has, but you have such a beautiful way of delivering your messages. And so, Awakened Healing, seven steps to renewed life. This is just a beautiful way to end our day one. I'm so grateful for you.

Nubbia Quezada: It's the steps in itself, or even just the word awakened healing, it really comes from a place where we are no longer hiding from our own shadow. It comes from a place where there's no more of that pointing game. It's really about taking ownership and finally realizing that you have a choice. We all have a choice to either stay where we're unhappy or unfulfilled, or we can decide to live every day as an opportunity.

This space came for me at a time when I thought that everything was going well. I truly can say that my entire life has been a gift in many ways because I was a rebellious kid, and I knew what I wanted. I always did what I felt was good for me, even if it meant that my parents were going to get upset at me or other people didn't agree with my decisions. The biggest growth for me was when I received my very first no, and this was recent. That put me in a space where I couldn't believe it. But at the same time, and I know a lot of people can relate to this, is that a lot of the decisions that we make unconsciously or even subconsciously, we do it in a space where there's a little bit of fear or the judgment or you're doing it out of a place of love, but it's as a cover-up. Let me explain. It's where we're doing something good to fill a void within ourselves. So always trying to help others, never saying no, always being that supporting hand. These are all great things, but then what are we hiding inside? Why are these things needed for us to feel good? Why aren't we feeling good within ourselves without having to do those things? For me, the moment someone said no to me, and made me realize that the things that I wanted to pursue were actually coming out of guilt. The guilt that I didn't even know was inside me, and it made me realize and reflect so much on my own life that it made me take many steps back to reflect and decide who I wanted to be. What's the type of person that I want to be? It's in that ability to choose who you want to be. It really comes down to that.

My brother is no longer with us. He suffered from mental illness. It's hard to even say it like this here; he took his life, and it was hard. It was really, really hard. But he was going through a really deep journey. There were lots of times when he was in a place where he was almost homeless. And he felt that he wasn't loved. And then he needed support when, as a family, if you know, or you deal with someone who has a mental illness, we love or give so much, but it's not received. It's not received, and they don't see it. There's just so much darkness that they can't even receive or even see the love that we're trying to give. In that space, I felt I had to do something. And I wanted to help bring him to wholeness in a way. But it was coming from a place where I needed something for me. So when they told me no, it was like, ugh, like a heartbreak. But then it made me realize that even though my intentions were good, that wasn't the direction that I was supposed to go.

Tracey Lee: It's all energy, right? This works in our businesses, too. When we really drop into our hearts, amazing things happen. When we're operating from our heads, we're disconnected, and people feel that you don't even need to say it. So that had to happen for you to realize and become awakened to something you weren't aware of. And then being able to ascertain that and then take that into a direction that feels more connected to your deeper self.

Nubbia Quezada: Absolutely. It's been quite the journey because even for me, where I stand and even what I do, it's this whole conscious awareness of being able to embrace our own spirit. And I think when it comes to harmonizing the mind, body, and soul, if one of the elements is not aligned or is being put to the side, there is no balance. And we're going to find chaos in our lives because we are neglecting that part. If you're spiritually sound, but you're neglecting the body side of things, maybe you're not taking care of or eating the right things that you should be eating. Or we are compromising our mental health with how we speak to ourselves. How are we nourishing our minds on a consistent basis?

The greatest gift I believe my brother could have given me is to connect with spirit. It was hard for me at first because I connected with my brother pretty much right after his funeral, or not a funeral, the mass service and being spiritually connected to him, I thought it was going to be that one time, but it wasn't. I connect with him daily but it's gone to a place where I'm now actually helping others connect with their loved ones in spirit, connect with their own soulfulness and their own love and purpose within themselves. And when we have that type of healing, the healing is not just about the pain but it's about what's residing within us. What are we actually hiding within us to pursue what we need to pursue? We have that, you know, clarity and alignment within ourselves. We can step in and be free of the judgment, the guilt, the shame, the anger, and all those things just kind of dissipate because we see life from a totally different perspective and we feel stuck in one area in our lives. It's actually holding us back because it's almost like a little anger, right?

Tracey Lee: Yeah, I want to help people understand this because I know you live this, and you feel this. Most people don't understand it, or they don't even know where to start connecting a body, mind, and soul. We want that trifecta, we want that connection. I think we can relate to the body, we can relate to the mind to a certain degree, and we can relate to the soul, but we're only scratching the surface. Honestly, I believe in all three areas, which is why most of us live at a very surface level, and this is why, hopefully, this summit is helping women start to realize going deeper is where the magic really lies, and that requires self-discovery work. So, with what you're doing and helping people connect to their spirits on a deeper level, can we talk about that and how that helps a woman get out of her way when she's feeling stuck and not moving forward? Maybe she's overcoming something, or maybe she's just wanting to step into something more. How do we connect with our spirit, first of all?

Nubbia Quezada: I think part of it is fear itself and diving into that unknown. Because we don't know what we're actually getting ourselves into even when someone says, "You are a spiritual being." Well, what does that even mean? What do you mean I'm a spiritual being? Even our ability to understand that concept can feel beyond us. Tapping into this connection that we have within ourselves requires practice and stillness. One example I can give is that I think everyone has done this. Have you ever walked into a room or you were thinking about something and there's too much noise and you forget about what you were thinking? Maybe the TV is on, and you say, can you just turn the TV off for a second? I just need to think about something, and as soon as they turn it off, it comes to you. I don't know if that's ever happened to you.

Tracey Lee: Oh yes, it just happened to me, I get impacted sometimes by a noise and my family asks, "What's wrong, Mom?" They all listen to their rock music and sometimes I feel like I can't even think when it's playing. I need calm to process my thoughts. So yes, I know exactly what you're talking about.

Nubbia Quezada: So, imagine if we did the same thing with our minds. As soon as we can be in a place where we can shut the chatter off, the mind allows us to actually feel and be present within ourselves. And that's hard for us to do.

Tracey Lee: Why is it so hard, though? I went out on the break, I lay down in the grass, and I just let the sunshine on me. It energized me in five minutes, that's all it took. I was starting to feel a little bit drained and I knew I needed to come back on and have high energy again. So why do we struggle with quieting our minds? Why do you think we struggle with that so much, Nubbia?

Nubbia Quezada: Well, it's definitely something that's been conditioned since we were kids. There are so many things requiring our attention. It's the TV, it's the play, it's the environment, it's the school. There was always something—over-scheduling. And it continues from school to high school, then you go to college or university. You've got to do this, you've got to get a job, and so it's like a constant role where it's like, whoa, when do we actually take a moment? Many people can relate, and I've done this myself in the past where we have even gone on vacation, and you don't even know what to do with yourself because you're used to being go, go, go, all the time.

Tracey Lee: Yeah, 100%, I have to discipline myself with that because I'm not good at what feels like slowing down. I find being in nature always helps.

Nubbia Quezada: Absolutely.

Tracey Lee: But it is crazy. You go on vacation, and you don't start to relax until you're halfway into your vacation.

Nubbia Quezada: Because your mind is constantly going. It requires practice to slow down the mind. Meditation is really good, but breathwork is even better, just sitting for a minute. I have a challenge I can give everybody to sit right now.

Tracey Lee: Can you take us through just a minute of stillness? I feel like everyone here could really use it. I feel that would be really beautiful. Are you able to do that for us?

Nubbia Quezada: Yeah, absolutely. If this does feel uncomfortable, it's okay. It's normal to have all those little feelings because you are asking your body to do something like just sitting. OK, now, close your eyes, and then I just want you to focus on your breath. Take each breath through your nose, make it nice and calm, and then release it through your mouth. Don't force anything, make this breath as natural as possible, even if you need to count on your own, like one, two, three in, and out at a count of three or four. However, you wish to breathe focusing on your breath because it allows you to be in the moment, allows you to recollect yourself, and be present in the moment. And if thoughts do come up, just acknowledge them and get back to your breath. How do you feel?

Tracey Lee: I feel so good—I feel grounded, I feel connected.

Nubbia Quezada: And that was just 90 seconds. The more you practice, you begin to really feel the benefits and it becomes a normal part of your day. And when you are in that present moment, you may receive little downloads that come in the form of ideas. It's just like this idea, this feeling, this inner knowing. This is where we can connect to our higher selves. When we shut our minds off and just be present. Our spirit, our soul, is what's actually speaking to us. And this space we've created allows us to listen.

Tracey Lee: I think we don't respect the downloads that come to us. We don't respect the beauty of that gift that's coming into our consciousness at that moment. My experience with women is most of the time, we just let them go. We don't allow them into the process. When you do listen, it could be something you want to follow through with in some way or take action on. This is how the summit came about. I was downloaded. I believe I was willed to do this by something greater than me. So was I connected to my spirit deeply at that time? Is that what was going on?

Nubbia Quezada: Absolutely, absolutely.

Tracey Lee: So good.

Nubbia Quezada: The thing is, once you hear, even just listening to me right now, whoever's listening, and it's not by accident if we can allow ourselves to be in a space where we can listen to ourselves, we will uncover so many things that you didn't even know existed.

I don't even know how to properly express the beauty of that. It's just the fact that we all have these abilities. It's just so profound and so just beautiful. Awakened. Very awakened. This is where that awakened healing comes. The moment you begin to do this, you start to heal old wounds. You start to see life through a whole different lens. And we start to hold, you know, compassion for ourselves. We've been doing that for others our entire lives. Now, we can be in a space where we can nurture ourselves because when we're good, our environment is good. The people around us are good.

Tracey Lee: We need to go back to school to learn how to hold ourselves. We literally need to go back to that. I think about all of you women and how we have trainers. We think of having a trainer for exercise.

Nubbia Quezada: Yeah, absolutely.

Tracey Lee: But we need trainers for our minds. We need trainers to connect with our souls. We need trainers to help us manage our money better and create our businesses. We truly need multifaceted ways of supporting us if we really want to live that holistic awakening life. Because the more awake you are, the more aware you are. And then you're able to receive these beautiful gifts that you keep getting downloaded. And the stillness, I mean, that is so simple, so powerful.

Nubbia Quezada: So simple and powerful, and something that everyone should be doing. It's not like this is not for me, I don't do that, or I've tried meditation, and it didn't work for me. Of course, it didn't, it's like you said, if you go to the gym or you apply for a new job, are you not going to be good at it when you first start? Nobody gets fit even in a month from working out. It takes time. You need to practice. You need to start eating better. You need to start drinking more water. Imagine you're giving yourself a gift. We have such a hard time taking care of all parts of who we are, not just one part, not just the two parts, it's all three parts—the mind, body, and spirit. And if we allow ourselves to experience our birthright, we were all born pure. We all have this innocence and this power within us. As we grow, things change not because of us but because of the things that we see— the environment, parenting—all those things. But when we get to a certain stage in our life, when we can actually decide and not allow our past to dictate who we are, it is just a part of our life. Now we can decide what is going to be the next script, and the best part is you can write it.

Tracey Lee: You can write it. And you know, you said something like, we are a powerful gift to ourselves. And I don't think we see ourselves as a gift. We see ourselves in the eyes of everybody else instead of seeing them through our eyes, like looking in the mirror and seeing ourselves for the first time. It's hard for a lot of women to look in the mirror and look at themselves. Very challenging. I know Mel Robbins did the High Five project and that is really simple. It's amazing how the simplest things are the things that truly have a massive impact. I think if we can shift our perspective on how we see ourselves and start to see ourselves as a gift, we start to be more awake to how we actually are supporting that gift. Are we allowing ourselves to say yes to the things that will support our healing? Can you talk about how you support women? Because I know you do some incredible work. Maybe share a story about a client that you've helped move through these seven steps to renewing her life through awakened healing. What does that look like? So we can understand a little bit more about how that works.

Nubbia Quezada: Yeah, absolutely. I mean, first things first, usually when anybody approaches me with our first call because I'm so intuitive and I get a lot of downloads right away, I can tell that there's a lot of masks being worn. And it's even one sharing, you know, about their life and all the things that they do, they're still holding back. I can just say one word, not that I want to make people cry, but it's just something that just hits inside where they realize that they're hiding and they're scared. They're trying to be someone for others and help others, especially being a mom or a wife or just someone in the work field where people depend on them. So, they're constantly playing all these roles. And they are lost, even though they feel like I'm doing this.

I've got this. So, really, what I do is take a step back. And let's view yourself. How do you actually view yourself? Like, I just told you, you just told me this, if I were to write this down. And you read it. What would you think about that person? And even just something so simple like that can really bring someone back and just be like, "Wow, I never really thought of it that way." And everyone is just so unique. What I do is harmonize the mind, body, and soul.

My background is in health and wellness, I can tap into that area of the body. However, on the spiritual side of things, I'm able to connect to their loved ones, and they connect with me to help guide them. So, through that practice, I give them the tools to practice, and there's a lot of journaling, there's meditation, and just allowing them to be present and not having an expectation. The moment they have an attachment to an expectation for a result, they have left the present moment.

Tracey Lee: We've left the heart, right? We're in the head.

Nubbia Quezada: Yeah, that's a blockage right there. That's not even an expectation that you even have for yourself. It actually trickles down with the expectations that we also have for others. And as soon as you let that go, that's when the magic happens.

Tracey Lee: Oh, it's so true. It happens, and all that freedom. I really feel like that's freedom.

Nubbia Quezada: Absolutely.

Tracey Lee: The world detached from all of that, that is true freedom.

Nubbia Quezada: It's in that space where a person, a woman, wants to be themselves, but they're seeing a different way from others, and they're scared to be who they are. And I get this a lot, even with their husbands. This is who my husband met. This woman has tried to be this, you know, wife and mother, but putting other things that truly mean a lot to her or even hiding parts of herself to be loved and accepted. And when we're living in that, we feel suffocated. And I think that's the hardest part. I'm a perfect example even for that as well, because as soon as I felt the confidence to even, this is who I am, this is what I want to pursue, this is I know what my heart is calling me to do. There's no one in the way. And this is not coming from a place of arrogance or anything like that. It's that knowing. And if anyone has anything to say, it is a projection of their own feelings, of their own fears. And as you're pursuing what you need to pursue, you will inspire people. You will be, "Wow, look at you go." And you start to embody that. You start to believe it yourself because you're seeing it. You know what I'm saying?

Tracey Lee: I'm just living it right now. I mean, I'm literally living that right now. I had no idea anyone wanted to come to this event, let alone be the speaker at this event. But I just had a deep understanding, all the things you're saying resonate with me on a deep spiritual level. I never felt more connected to the decision to do this summit. I felt it physically, emotionally, everything. It propelled me, and it's the only way to create the life that you want, renew who you are today, and become a better person tomorrow. That's been my personal experience.

You are a powerful soul. I love that you took us through that beautiful breathwork and I so appreciate you, Nubbia. I appreciate your calmness, I appreciate your honesty, I appreciate your story. It's just been really fun having you as a part of this summit. We needed you in this summit. We need you in this summit because we're all so different. We're so diverse, and we need all of this throughout, and this is the beautiful thing. I always see this holistic wheel. We're all locking arms, we're all different. You know, we all come from different pasts, and we all have different gifts, but all of us are working in harmony together and sharing the gifts we have. And for you to help us awaken to those gifts, I am grateful, I am grateful, I am grateful. Thank you, thank you, thank you.

Nubbia Quezada: Thank you. I feel so honored and blessed to be here and to be able to share. And there's this, all these emotions kind of come up, but I'm finally living my purpose and what I am doing.

Tracey Lee: Virtual hug for you. You rounded up this day amazingly.

To watch Tracey Lee's interview with Nubbia Quezada, scan the QR Code below.

Angeline Constantinou

Founder and CEO of Let's Break the Silence with Angeline LLC

https://www.linkedin.com/in/angelinemitchell/
https://www.facebook.com/angeline.constantinou/
https://www.instagram.com/angeline_constantinou/
https://www.letsbreakthesilence.com

Angeline Constantinou is the Founder and CEO of Let's Break the Silence with Angeline LLC. Angeline is dedicated to helping women who have suffered domestic abuse regain their power and acquire the necessary tools to heal and embrace goodness and love in their lives.

Having experienced similar struggles, Angeline understands the journey firsthand and is determined to provide guidance and community so women can thrive and be victorious in their lives.

The pivotal moment in Angeline's life came when she made the courageous decision to leave an abusive ex-husband, a step that marked her transition from victim to victor.

Since then, she has embarked on a path of personal growth, crafting a new plan and establishing a community built on trust and security. Through this process, she discovered that she was not alone on her journey.

Today, Angeline collaborates with remarkable women communities, including the Millionaire Mentorship group, where she hosts webinars and serves as a guest speaker on influential platforms such as the Pink Panther Podcast, Inspired News Radio, The Change Book Podcast and Women 4 Women Radio Network in Canada

Her diverse experiences and personal growth journey have led Angeline to establish her own coaching business, specializing in supporting women as they navigate the transition from overwhelming confusion to confidence.

From Breakdown to Breakthrough

By Angeline Constantinou

TRACEY & JENN MOMENTS

Jenn Iannuzzi: Day two, day two. How are you feeling, Tracey? How are you feeling?

Tracey Lee: I need some beats. Oh my gosh. I'm so excited. Honestly, there were so many magical moments yesterday. So many. Honestly, I came into this thinking it was going to be a really beautiful day. I had no idea how these speakers were going to show up as powerfully as they did, the things that they shared, the conversations that were had, the golden nuggets that were dropped, like, seriously.

Jenn Iannuzzi: So much vulnerability, too? I think that was the thing that really got me. I mean, I must have cried three times yesterday.

Tracey Lee: Yeah. And you know what? That's because this is deep work, like the stuff we're talking about. This is real stuff. You can't hide from what we're talking about. This is bringing it out, putting it on the table, and giving us something to really resonate with. I mean, when you resonate with something, you feel connected to it. You know, someone might say something, and you're like, oh my gosh, I feel that. You watch a movie, and you cry, right? You hear lyrics to a song and you feel it in your heart and your soul.

Jenn Iannuzzi: I think we could all see ourselves in each of the speakers, you know, their stories were so powerful. They just really resonated. I mean, I can't even imagine what today's going to bring.

Tracey Lee: Oh my gosh. Yeah, we have an incredible lineup.

Jenn Iannuzzi: Before we do that. Should we talk through some of the key takeaways from yesterday?

Tracey Lee: Yeah, Oh, I definitely want to do that. We started with Shae. She's a force to be reckoned with, that beautiful girl. And she really helped us understand reclaiming what's ours.

Jenn Iannuzzi: Radical responsibility. Those words, I swear to God, I'm going to put them above my computer.

Tracey Lee: We have to take radical responsibility, nobody else is going to do that for us. And yes, that was radical when I made shifts in my life. Radical departures of behavior were the only way that I could seriously elevate where I needed to go and create the new results I wanted. Radical departures of behaviors and making radical decisions are what helped to get to a radical quantum leap. And she is living that. I've been blessed to be living that. We have to stop waiting for life to tell us when it's our time.

Jenn Iannuzzi: Start building your queendom, right? I just love that word. And then we moved into Christina.

Tracey Lee: Oh yeah, Christina. Oh my gosh.

Jenn Iannuzzi: She talked about how dreaming isn't just for kids.

Tracey Lee: No, dreaming is not just for kids. It's for adults and we deserve what Christina said that she wasn't risking anything when she was staying comfortable. She wasn't in the habit of taking risks, and when she took her first risk, all of a sudden, things started to shift, her energy shifted, and new ideas and opportunities came in. And she recognized the value of taking risks and taking a chance on herself. She did that. And defying doubters, like understanding that defy means not obeying. That's not obeying people who are trying to tell us we can't do what we want to do.

And then we had Margaret, beautiful Margaret. Oh my gosh, seriously, the thing she dropped about grief and how to show up and how to support and understand what grief really is, whoa, that was really big.

Jenn Iannuzzi: I had no idea—I really didn't. And you know, now I just like having that knowledge to be able to show up for our friends and family members who are grieving in a nonjudgmental way. Her story was so impactful in her teachings, too. I really took that to heart, and I got on the phone with my mother, and we had a conversation afterward.

Tracey Lee: Oh, that's beautiful, Jenn. Oh my gosh, that's amazing. Yes, this is the power of women sharing their gifts. Understand that you all have gifts, and if we don't share those gifts, we aren't supporting you. These women are sharing their gifts that are impacting hundreds of women who will impact other women and other people in their lives. This is why we can't sit silent with our gifts. The world needs what you have.

Then we had Nubia, who closed up the day with her awakening healing and took us to a beautiful breathwork moment, which I loved. It wasn't planned, but I just felt like, let's bring this into everybody and give ourselves that still moment.

Jenn Iannuzzi: We all needed it at that point, we really did, and it was a great moment.

Tracey Lee: The stillness was so beautiful. So, we have four powerful speakers coming on today. We have an incredible woman starting and kicking us off. Why don't you share with this beautiful community today, Jenn, who Angeline is what she is all about?

Introduction

Meet Angeline Mitchell, the driving force behind "Let's Break the Silence with Angeline." Her mission is deeply personal, born from her own journey through the shadows of domestic abuse into the light of self-empowerment. Angeline's work is not just about helping survivors;

it's about building a stigma-free world where women can thrive together, rewriting their stories with hope and endless possibilities. She's the change-maker who's turned her breakdown into a breakthrough, and she's here to guide others to do the same.

Angeline's life is a blend of bold decisions and heartfelt passions. If she could afford any car, she'd be driving a Porsche—an emblem of her bold and determined spirit. But despite her boldness, she's also cautious in some ways, preferring to dip a toe into the pool before cannonballing in.

Angeline grew up in Minnesota but now calls New York home, a city that matches her bold energy and relentless drive. Her favorite pastime is podcasting, where she shares her insights, stories, and vision with the world. And when it comes to relaxation, she's all about a long nap in the midday, recharging to continue her important work.

Her hero? Tony Bennett, a figure who, much like Angeline, exemplifies resilience and grace. She loves quoting *Gone with the Wind*, perhaps for its themes of strength and survival. If she could be transformed into any animal, it would be a lion—fierce, courageous, and powerful, just like she is.

Angeline's tastes are as unique as her journey. Her favorite dessert is crème brûlée, and she starts her mornings with oatmeal and berries, a fresh and healthy choice that mirrors her preference for fresh food over fried. If she ever had to change her name, she'd choose Angelica, a name that captures the essence of her spirit.

Street-smart and a firm believer in learning by doing, Angeline's journey has been anything but ordinary. She's someone who regrets very little but does mention that spending money on her divorce is something she wishes she could take back—a testament to the painful yet transformative experiences that have shaped her. Her favorite body part? Her butt, a playful nod to self-confidence and embracing who she is.

But what makes Angeline truly hopeful is her vision—a vision for a world where survivors of domestic abuse can step out of the shadows and into the light, empowered and ready to rewrite their stories. As you get to know Angeline, you'll see a woman who is not just surviving but thriving, and she's here to make sure others do the same.

INTERVIEW

Tracey Lee: I was so excited that you were starting off the day because I feel your energy every time we talk.

Angeline Mitchell: Thank you.

Tracey Lee: Oh, this is amazing. How are you feeling?

Angeline Mitchell: Feeling refreshed and recharged. I had a great night's sleep. Yeah, ready to go.

Tracey Lee: Ready to go, so good.

Angeline Mitchell: Fired up, pumped up, how's that?

Tracey Lee: You guys are in for a treat. This woman, I mean, honestly, you are so friggin' passionate. You ooze passion. Passion for your purpose, passion for helping people, passion for showing up and just continuing to push through and breaking down all the barriers that keep showing up. You really are unstoppable. You're incredible. And I'm just so blessed that I met you.

Angeline Mitchell: I am blessed that we met, too. I remember when we talked about this in June, and this was right after I came back from Chicago. I said, you know what? I'm all in. I invested in myself because I know what it takes to get out of your own damn way. I know what it feels like going through the throes of a divorce, going through half of my adult life with domestic violence, and feeling ashamed. And things just spiraled downward for me. I was married for half of my adult life.

Tracey Lee: Wow.

Angeline Mitchell: Yeah, at 25.

Tracey Lee: And you know what, your story, that defining moment where you were downloaded with an idea. You grabbed your phone, and you did something, so I wonder if you even had control over that moment. It was decided for you, and you just, literally, leaned into it and did something that was very, very courageous. Can you share with all these incredible women what happened? I know these are the kinds of moments that we need to hear because we can resonate with them in our own lives in our own way to help us find the courage to say, "Ah, I'm going to do this." So share your story, share what happened in that moment, Angeline.

Angeline Mitchell: Yes, what happened at that moment was that I hired a mentor back in 2017 because I was still struggling with breaking through my self-limiting beliefs even though I broke free from domestic violence fourteen and a half years ago, which I'm very proud of. Once upon a time, I was married to who I thought was the love of my life and we earned a six-figure income in New York City. I was the one who brought in the money, But then, one day, he physically abused me. I was in the hospital. I had to have reconstructive nose surgery. And I felt ashamed to share my story. That pivoting moment for me when I hired my mentor, he said, you know, you're close to your breakthrough. However, you have not shared your story with the world live on Facebook. And I was like, oh, I could do that. I used to be the biggest chicken of going live on Facebook.

In March, I took my phone and hit live and shared my story of how I went from victim to claiming victory in my life from domestic violence. And at that moment in time, the live went viral. Seven million views later. That means seven million people were impacted by my story because it was brutal. I went through a breakdown. When I tell you that things spiraled downwards, I mean I lost money and was nearly financially bankrupt. He wrote out balance transfer checks against our credit because it was in both names, so he could buy mutual funds fifty thousand dollars worth. I found myself in a really, really bad dark place fourteen and a half years ago. I had every reason to give up, just play the pity party. I was curled up in bed. I'm saying, what do I do? What should I do? And I was so afraid. I felt so ashamed. So, I woke up one morning with an epiphany. I called my attorney, which a good friend of mine recommended. And I drove down to her office and wrote out a check for $5,000 to start divorce proceedings. That was the pivoting moment for me. When I wrote out that check and shared my story on Facebook, because guess what? People are looking for hope, especially women, and, as women, we need to rise up. It took a lot of faith and belief. I prayed. I mean, I turned to God for guidance. Just think about it for a minute.

You can only be in survival mode and victim mode for so long. So, I finally rose up. I claimed. I surrendered. I said, screw this, and I wrote out a check against my own credit card because I had a credit card in my own name. So, I said I'm just going to write out the check, and that's it. I had no money. I had like $25 in my purse, enough to get me down to New York because I used to live in Rhinebeck. It was a 20-minute drive for me. I was broke, and I was homeless. I was living like a gypsy for one year. I shared my story with the world because someone needs to hear this. I have always been passionate about helping women find and amplify their voices. So, that pivoting moment for me, seven million views later, my life went all over the world. It went to the United Kingdom, South Africa, Europe, and the US. It was viral. I don't even remember how many shares I had for that Live. It probably was 10,000 shares because when I woke up the next morning, I was shaking. And you're talking to a person here who was afraid to go live. You're talking to a person who was shaking, you know, how it is like when you hold the camera. I had no tripod at the time because it was just that block that I had, but whatever. So imagine holding your camera and looking at the camera. I'm shaking. I'm sharing my story, and there are over a hundred people on my Facebook page already watching me live. It just went ding ding ding ding ding and people shared it out. That live had such a ripple effect. The best investment that I made was paying my mentor $2,000. And I was working in corporate America at the time. So I used my paycheck, my bonus check to do that. So you see what happens?

Tracey Lee: This is one of the most powerful stories I've ever heard. And it is going to give so many people hope beyond belief and understanding, you're not meant to go through anything in life alone. You're not meant to celebrate alone, you're not meant to deal with grief alone, you're not meant to go through the challenges that you went through by yourself. We are not meant to, and not only are we not meant to, we can't. And you were guided by that mentor in your life to give you that challenge. You took it on, and look what happened and now, not only in that moment but since then you're now helping hundreds of women get through and break their breakdowns and create their breakthroughs and get out of victimhood and be victorious. We freaking love you.

Angeline Mitchell: Ah, I freaking love you for having me here.

Tracey Lee: You're so incredible. Look what your voice did to help. This is what the world needs. The world needs the stuff we don't think is good enough to offer or even share. How can we even think we know that we have to just take a chance on ourselves? You took a chance on yourself. You could have stayed homeless, you could have all these things happened, but you had something rooted in you that was like no, and one person changed your life.

Angeline Mitchell: That's all it takes: making that investment in yourself. By the way, I invested my bonus check, which was $2,000, which I just said I was going to put back into myself and pour all of that investment into myself because my mentor knew that my breakthrough was around the corner.

He knew it.

Tracey Lee: Yeah.

Angeline Mitchell: He knew it. He says your breakthrough is around the corner.

Tracey Lee: He felt you wanted it so bad.

Angeline Mitchell: When you want something so bad, you will get it. You will achieve it no matter what because I suffered financially, and I was addicted to suffering for way too long. That's the human condition. Especially for women who are going through domestic violence. They are addicted to suffering. When you're sick and tired of being the victim, there's something inside of you that is going to break through. They've been conditioned to feel worthless. They've already been conditioned to lack self-worth and self-confidence. I mean, literally, these ladies have been pounded down to the ground. They've been pounded down to the ground. So, for me, see, I wanted to change and get out in the first place.

Tracey Lee: So how do we build up? We recognize this is the situation we're in. We recognize it, we're addicted to these emotions, okay? So, we have awareness, we're willing to accept that that is our current circumstances, right? Sometimes, we don't want to even acknowledge that this is our current circumstances. And until you acknowledge that and look at yourself and go, okay, this is where I'm at right now. I need to be honest with myself—direct, loving, and honest. Now, as a woman, what do we do next, Angeline? How do we start to build our life back up? Where do we go? Like dealing with the fears. There must be acute fear. But knowing that you took faith and overcame your fear, how do you help women do that?

Angeline Mitchell: Well, I help women through self-discovery. It's a process. So, let's fast-forward to that. I have invested over $50,000 in myself in personal development and personal growth, and I recently got my life coaching certification from the ACLU. So, basically, I took the bull by the horns, and I said, I'm just going to surrender, and I am going to put in the work. I allied myself with mentors and coaches who believed in me. I'm so grateful for that. I decided to build a side hustle for myself. At that time, it was in the health and fitness industry. And my coach, who brought me on, was very supportive of my story and everything. So, I did what I had to do. I built my business behind the scenes because I wanted it. The alternative is to feel sorry for yourself and not do anything. That is the worst thing you can do. I invested in personal growth and personal development. A year later, after the divorce became final one month later, I flew to Los Angeles, California, for a summit. I can tell you that was life-changing. I met MJ Durkin. I met so many great people. I had a blast, and I said, you know what? I can live on my own and support myself. To this day, I am financially independent, and I have a course and a membership program for domestic violence survivors because I want to help them move into healing, move from that lost, depressed, overwhelmed state into healing, empowerment, and thrive. Healing together, thriving forever. I can tell you, it's a journey, a self-discovery journey.

You learn a lot about yourself. Oh boy, I realized that I could go out to dinner by myself. I could go out on a date by myself. I don't need a man to make me happy. Love yourself. That's the biggest thing about loving yourself because when you love yourself, you are able to love others. The worst thing you can do is feel sorry for yourself. I did that. I mean, that was for too many years. But anyway, yes, that is the worst thing you can do is feel sorry for yourself or just curl up in the bed and wait for things to happen. It's not going to happen. You have to put in the work. I had to break through those self-limiting beliefs. I had to do mirror work. I mean, you have no idea what I had to do. And once I was able to do that and share my story, the world of abundance opened up. You attract all the good in your life because, like attracts like, if you're putting out negative to the universe, you're going to attract negative people in your life. When you put out good, you give more than you receive. So when you give to people, it comes back.

It's a ripple effect.

Tracey Lee: It is a ripple effect. Okay, so what I'm hearing from you, what got you out of your circumstances, was being open to receiving the support, open to asking, and then receiving support from another person who was brought to you to support you. Without that, you probably would still be worse. I recognize the power of that, and you've stepped into now serving women to support them because you believe nobody else should be stuck in those situations. That is like when you talk about your life force, talk about using something for the greater good. So, going back to that moment when you didn't think you had a choice, what would you say to those women right now who are in an abusive relationship, who probably feel shame and blame, maybe they have children in that relationship, who knows? What would you say to that woman right now who is facing you? What would you share with her?

Angeline Mitchell: Well, I would share with her my story, and then I would share that there's hope, there's light at the end of the tunnel. In fact, there was a woman when COVID hit, and I started my podcast two months before, not knowing that COVID would happen. A woman reached out to me. And she was crying. She felt helpless and crying, crying, crying. And then, finally, she calmed down. And, you know, I'm the type of coach who tells it straight up. I don't beat around the bush. You kind of have to play the doctor a little bit and dive into what's causing them to feel this way. So, a month later, I said, there is a homeless shelter in New York City. I used to live in New York City. I worked in New York City. I earned a six-figure income. I went through the throes of divorce in New York City, which is not easy because the court system is whatever it is. But I did tell her there are resources—go to your local office, go to me, you know, and she did it. I gave her a direction.

Tracey Lee: Yes, yes, and what was there for her was always there. She just couldn't frickin' see it because she was so stuck in her victimhood, shame, blame, and all the negative stuff was overpowering her every day. She couldn't see what was right there for her to help pull her out. So you directed her, wow.

Angeline Mitchell: That's right, I directed her all right.

Tracey Lee: It's so amazing, Angeline. You gave a voice to the voiceless with that woman. She realized she had a choice, and she always had a choice. When you finally realize that and you try out using your voice and your choice, what happens? You get it, you experience something you didn't experience before, and it gives you more hope.

Angeline Mitchell: Right, exactly. So, now she's living. She escaped, and she has a child too. I think they found a studio apartment for her. That's having a roof over your head. So you see that? That was her breakthrough.

Angeline Mitchell: One week from today, I'm going to be on a plane to San Diego for a women's conference. And I am a co-author of a book series that is going to be released, God willing, next week or the week after. It is going out to 30 countries.

Tracey Lee: Angeline, we're in this to win for you beautiful souls. I appreciate you. I am so grateful for this new friendship we have, and I'm just grateful for what you do every single day. Thank you. Thank you. Thank you.

Angeline Mitchell: I'm grateful for you, Tracey. Thank you.

To watch Tracey Lee's interview with Angeline Mitchell, scan the QR Code below.

Ariel Jarvis

Vitality Wellness World

https://www.linkedin.com/in/ariel-jarvis-803410281/
https://www.facebook.com/vitalityHW
https://www.instagram.com/vitality_wellness_/
https://www.vitalitywellnessw.com/
http://www.vitalitywellnesswater.com/

By trade, Ariel Jarvis is a registered Natural Health Practitioner, Herbalist, Nutritionist, Microscopist, Iridologist, & Acutherapist. At her clinic Vitality Wellness World, she dives deep with each patient to discover the root cause of health concerns. Ariel helps her patients take control of their health with customized protocols, bio-hacking and optimizing on the cellular level. She has a passion for the deaf and is one of very few health care workers fluent in ASL and committed to making a difference in that community. Outside of the office, Ariel is highly social and loves spending her free time with friends and family. She is passionate about fitness and works hard in the gym on her fitness goals. Ariel loves sharing about health with others, speaking on stages, podcasts, and social media about all things mindset, health, wellness, and motivation. In Ariel's words, "Being healthy and fit isn't a trend, it's a lifestyle!

Biohacking Your Way to a Better Life

By Ariel Jarvis

Meet Ariel, the ultimate guide to biohacking your way to a better life. A rare blend of financial expertise and holistic health mastery, Ariel is a force to be reckoned with in both the worlds of wealth management and wellness. She juggles multiple ventures, including a unique wealth-care program that ensures your assets are just as healthy as your body. With titles like Herbalist, Nutritionist, and Accu-Therapist under her belt, Ariel dives deep—right down to the cellular level—to craft personalized health protocols that address your specific needs.

But Ariel's talents don't stop there. Her heart beats especially strongly for the deaf community, where she bridges the wellness gap with her fluency in American Sign Language. Whether she's ensuring your wealth is in prime shape or optimizing your health with the right antioxidants, Ariel's approach is as comprehensive as it is compassionate.

Ariel's personal life is just as fascinating. She describes her style in one word: "Classy mother." Despite being tech-savvy, she's clear that her passions lie more with holistic wellness than gadgets. And though she's a social butterfly who enjoys performing in front of an audience, she treasures her alone time—especially when it's spent with her dog, who is her guilty pleasure.

Ariel is motivated by the desire to expand herself as a human being, always pushing the boundaries of her knowledge and capabilities. She's learned many lessons along the way, but one that took her time to master was the art of surrendering—a lesson that has no doubt influenced her holistic approach to life.

When it comes to the little things, Ariel's choices are just as telling. Her favorite music? Classical. Her favorite movie genre? Romance. In the summer, you'll find her swimming, one of her favorite pastimes. And if she could choose between traveling to the past or the future, she'd choose the future—always looking ahead, much like her approach to life and wellness.

Ariel's love for the forest reflects her connection to nature, and she prefers flying over driving, perhaps because it allows her to look at the world from a higher perspective—both literally and figuratively. She's not afraid to tackle challenges head-on, even if that means killing bugs she finds inside or making the difficult choice to surrender when necessary.

As you get to know Ariel, you'll see that she's more than just a financial whiz or a holistic health maven. She's a woman who is deeply committed to expanding herself and those around her, ensuring that every aspect of life—whether it's wealth, health, or personal growth—is in peak condition. Get ready to be inspired by Ariel's story, and perhaps learn a few biohacks of your own along the way.

INTERVIEW

Tracey Lee: Yay! I'm giving you a big hug. I'm hugging you right now virtually, and the day we actually do it in person is going to be explosive. I can't wait for that moment.

Ariel Jarvis: I know, I know, we literally keep talking about this. And I feel like I'm just getting so excited for the finale, just being able to do that. I know because we built such a beautiful bond over the phone—a virtual bond. And so when we finally see each other, it's going to be electric.

Tracey Lee: It already is electric when we're together. And we've been together in moments like this many, many times because we both have this beautiful passion for helping others in a way that for us was beginning with health. But I want to just take a moment because I know you're going to share some wisdom with us. That will be incredibly moving and wake us up on levels that we're not awake to right now. But before I do that, you know, in the essence of this incredible summit and moving forward so we can move others, I want to acknowledge how you moved, and you continue to move yourself. You don't accept the things that aren't working, you are the queen of **not accepting** your BS. Ariel, it truly doesn't matter what comes your way, you always overcome it. You have a mindset of "I will always overcome it because it doesn't have to stay this way." I love that so much!!!!

Tracey Lee: That is a powerful strength you have inside of you that has allowed you to do things. I don't even know if we have enough time to share all the things that you get your hands on. Sometimes, you must get dirty to help other people the way you help them, but you do this because your heart is so huge.

Ariel Jarvis: I really appreciate you, too. I just adore you, and I love you, and I'm so grateful that we were able to get connected and be able to help and share and inspire and empower other women because the more we work together and the more we collaborate, we get rid of all of the competition, jealousy, dysfunction, baggage, and all of a sudden we create a wave. We create a huge tsunami of confidence and power. Never underestimate the change that is created when women come together. This is the impact society needs right now, but first, we have to change ourselves and we have to change our mindset because it is a battlefield. What people don't realize is you can have the stamina to do all the amazing things you are capable of when life is good, but let me see if you have the same stamina or stronger when you're at your knees. That's what I want to know. I want that grit. And that grit you can't get from a book or a pill, that grit comes from life when you keep getting knocked down. And you just have to put a smile on your face, be a little bit ferocious, and become a savage.

Tracey Lee: Savage for your dreams, savage for your beliefs, savage for your vision.

Ariel Jarvis: Yes. Savage for love, savage for change, savage for the hug you didn't get. You have to be your own damn hero.

Tracey Lee: Yeah, you really do have to be your biggest cheerleader, you know. We cheerlead other people, and we also cheerlead our excuses, and they're right in there inside of us. And we hold on to the reasons why we think we can't do something. When women tell me their "I can't" list, I ask them how they feel when they share this and if that is the outcome they really want. Not achieving the thing they desire. It's always an 'aha' moment. Our highest self is our best and biggest hero. That was one of the Rapid Fire questions: Who's your hero? I know people celebrate other people, and I love that, but turn that back into you and be a hero for yourself. That's amazing, Ariel.

Okay, you did a post a while ago and I think I messaged you right away. I'm like, okay, I love everything you just said. And it was really you being so present, working through stuff, stepping on top of the pile, and frigging crushing it. Not from a masculine place, but from a powerful feminine energy that is like you don't get to mess with me anymore kind of place. And you shared five really powerful pillars and I want everyone to have their pens right now. I'm going to write these down. So I want you to share these with us, Ariel, and I want you to elaborate on them in a way that we can take them and start to implement some small shifts into our own lives today.

Ariel Jarvis: Get your pens ready because these five core values are things that I operate from. And for me, it's not just about quality of life, but it's also about living an extraordinary life. I don't want an average life. There's nothing wrong with an average life. It's just there's something inside of me. And I know there's something inside of you that says, I want more. Not in a selfish greedy way. But you want your life to matter in a way where it's like, some people don't get the opportunity to wake up every day. But I did. And you did. And we're living and breathing, but we're taking it for granted. We're not maxing out our day. We're too busy, you know, making up excuses, living through our traumas, carrying all this unnecessary baggage that is in the past. No one cares about what you're going through. The show must go on. So, you need to do a deep dive into the ability to overcome your challenges but have it with grace, love, and joy. You don't need to do it miserably. You need to go through the pain with peace and you need to go through it with love.

So, the five core values I abide by are. As a natural health practitioner, I take these steps very seriously. I don't compromise, and other people might say it's extreme, but I feel better now than I ever have because I don't compromise with my health. For me, it's all about having a strong body, so I train three hours a day. I do triathlons and marathons, and I've done bodybuilding competitions where I went against women that were on steroids, and I was completely, you know, with no steroids. I've done 12 years as a prima ballerina. I got all my RAD, I became a classical ballet teacher. I've done so much. I've gotten into so many different classical ballet shows and big names, but what I learned in that was how to discipline my mind and my body and get my body to do things that were uncomfortable to push through that lactic acid and be able to push through that burn. I can just walk out of the gym and go home. No one's forcing me to be there, I'm forcing myself to be there because I'm building strength, I'm building grit, and I'm pushing past that pain. So, that's one thing you need to learn. You need to push your body in some sort of physical activity that your body will allow without harming. But there are different types of pain, and you need to learn how to push yourself. We are designed to be machines.

The second one is you need to have a strong mind. Very important because, like we said, some things are going to hit you when you're already down. You might lose a baby. Your husband might walk out on you. You might lose a million dollars. You might lose your business. You might lose your reputation and your respect. You might lose your health. You might get cancer. Your whole family could die, or the whole world could shut down. Who knows? But your mind is everything. No one can steal your peace unless you give it up for free.

The third one is, where are you spiritually? Are you connected to the divine? Or are you just walking around like a sack of flesh, you know, just consuming, consuming, consuming? You can't take it to heaven. And there's one thing that I've learned is sometimes the supernatural has to come in and they have to do things that people would say are miracles. I've had many many miracles happen that I can't even explain, and I would have to say I give it all to God.

Number four, finance people don't realize that financial trauma can affect you forever. It can also be passed down to generations because if you came from a family where maybe they didn't have enough money, maybe your parents split, maybe you had a single mom. Who knows your story? Everyone comes into the world, typically poor and broke. But if you die poor and broke, that's on you because there is abundance around you and there is so much opportunity.

And the fifth one is our emotions. Don't let your emotions lead or dictate your life. Oh, if it feels happy, do it. Hell no. Sometimes, I just want to sit at home and not go to the gym, but I'm going to go to the gym anyway, even if my legs are burning and I'm not even there yet. Or I'm going to go for a 30k run, even though I feel like my ankle's a little bit bugged up. It's all about training that grit. People let their emotions dictate how they run their lives instead of letting logic dictate, or there's a lot of assuming that happens. Oh, they're saying this about me, they think that about me. I'm like, did you ask them? Is that what they said? Is that what they did? Oh, well, the family thinks this of me. Stop putting words in people's mouths and stop playing a record in your own head about yourself. That's not even true. Have you ever asked somebody what they actually think about you, someone who loves you and respects you? I bet you that the record that they're saying is completely different from the record you're playing.

Tracey Lee: Oh, absolutely.

Ariel Jarvis: Get that record out of your head. Start pouring into yourself because here's the thing: Your body runs on a vibration. I have a biophysics biochemistry background. Your body has about 75 trillion cells. Every single cell runs at 70 millivolts. Your body runs at a certain frequency for healing and for the parasympathetic state, which is rest and digestion. But did you know that emotions are our energy in motion, their energy? Every single emotion has its own frequency. Just like when you play a piano, every note has its own frequency. We have about 76,000 thoughts a day on average in our subconscious. And whatever we constantly replay, your body feels that. That emotion and energy go into your cells and your nervous system and create something called cell memory in your cell blueprint. Your cells turn over every 25 days on average, making a whole new generation of cells based on what you eat, drink, and your cell blueprint. Your cell blueprint can be biohacked. It's not just what you eat, what you drink, what you put in your body. It's also the energy that you consume, the people you spend your time with, and the things you listen to on social media and TV. Fear, anger, frustration, and worry will make you sick.

Tracey Lee: They're the lowest vibration. If you understand that, all of those things that we continue to play in our minds and feed, right? Through different things in our minds and the minute we leave the present moment, that's when we experience fear. That's when we allow these things to come running in our head because right now you're safe, I'm safe, we're here, we're present, but the minute we start thinking about this or that, then all of a sudden, we leave the present moment, and that's where all that shit lives. That shit is all those emotions.

Somebody said earlier that money follows joy because joy is the highest, right? That's where we feel this beautiful experience like I think of when my son, my first child, was born. I was adopted, and I had no one in my life who was blood-connected. And when he was born, I remember, I can't even put words to that kind of joy, right? The emotion was like the feeling, like the body's vibrating, right? And that vibration goes out beyond you. It's so beautiful, Ariel. And I think if we could just bottle that and, like, intravenously inject it, but that's not how it works because it has to work from our heart, right?

Ariel Jarvis: I know what people don't realize is you can hack that because your brain has something called a neurological pathway.

Tracey Lee: How do we do this?

Ariel Jarvis: Okay, so I'm just going to repeat myself. You have about 75 trillion cells in your body and your cells turn over on average about 25 days based on what you eat, drink, and your cell blueprint. Your cell blueprint has a cell memory. That cell memory is what makes the next generation of cells come. Those weaknesses you have will get passed on to the next cell cycle. So, what we do is: we sit down together, we do an analysis, we do blood work, we'll do a whole body scan, all this cool stuff, and we'll actually be able to take a look at your cell blueprint and look at your weaknesses. Then, based on your emotional vectors, we do a whole emotional body scan with neuro biohacking. And then, throughout the 11 body systems, we can identify any variable creating inflammation, imbalance, dysfunction, infection, or deficiency within that body system on a cellular level.

Tracey Lee: Wow. What are the 11 body systems?

Ariel Jarvis: So you have your, I won't say them in exact chronological order, nervous system, cardiovascular system, urinary tract, digestion, intestinal, reproductive system, urinary system, cell blueprint, and your immune system. I don't have them all listed, but it goes on and on.

Tracey Lee: That's a lot.

Ariel Jarvis: It's a lot.

Tracey Lee: Wow. We don't think of our bodies as a system that works in harmony together, and I think we lose respect for our bodies. You are like the complete extreme of how you support your body. But understanding, I know, is what gives us that fuel to say, okay, now I get it, now I can see it. When I make the choices I make, I have an understanding of what the consequence is going to be and what the long-term impact could be if I keep doing this. So, I have a choice to make. I have a decision to make. And that's when you've reclaimed your power back, right? Reclaiming your power back with your health.

Ariel Jarvis: And I tell people, you don't have to be perfect. I tell people that when we're doing a reset or a biohack, we need to get all of our main health concerns back into check. We need to let that now go into the new cell blueprint. Just like when you do renovations for your kitchen, you're changing the foundation, you're changing the blueprint. Well, what we're doing is we're changing the blueprint. We have to be extreme when we're doing the internal work. But when we get things back into alignment, we do the 80/20 rule because I still want you to go out and live your life, but we don't want to slide back into that inflammation. So that's where I say pick your poison, don't pick too many, don't do it too often, reset often, and listen to your body. Your body can't send you a text or an email. It will let you know through signs of inflammation or if one of those 11 body systems is not functioning properly.

Tracey Lee: Okay, I want to go back to those things you just said so everyone can write those down because it just rolls off you like lava, like your symphony. I didn't know you were a ballerina. That's really cool, wow yeah. I think I'm a ballerina in my head, I do, I believe I can do it. Okay, and maybe one day I will.

Ariel Jarvis: I will show you, yes.

Tracey Lee: Okay, so go down those things. The first thing you said was what? Not the core values. What were you just saying?

Ariel Jarvis: Core.

Tracey Lee: You just shared a whole list of things you need to do—this, this, this, and this. Now, I've lost my train of thought. It was important.

Ariel Jarvis: Get the replay.

Tracey Lee: What were you just sharing? It was just so fast. Okay, it'll come back to me. Okay, way through the cells in the blueprint. And then you said the phrase…

Ariel Jarvis: You want to pick your poison.

Tracey Lee: Your poison. What do you mean by that? Like coffee?

Ariel Jarvis: It could be coffee. It could be eating past seven. It could be overeating once in a while. Your stomach is the size of your fist, and you only make enough enzymes, hydrochloric acid, and pepsin to break down the surface area of your fist. So, if you overeat, you're stretching the stomach. The stomach is a muscle, which means it can't contract properly. So now you're going to get undigested food going into the small and large intestine, and the bad MAC microbes, parasites, fungus, mold, and Candida viruses are feeding on that undigested food, creating inflammation in the entire body. So don't overeat. Our society is all about overeating. Don't do that.

So, pick your poison. Don't pick too many. Don't do the poison too often. And reset often when you feel out of alignment. It's really easy to do those quick little fixes. But if you ignore it and it goes on for too long, then it makes the work a lot harder. I would love it if we could get to the point where you don't have the autoimmune and the cancer. That means that it's now chronic. And now it's going to take us a lot longer, and you have to be disciplined a lot longer. But if we're dealing with, say, maybe a little bit of weight gain or we're dealing with a little bit of insomnia or maybe some headaches or maybe a little bit of joint pain, but we don't have a true diagnosis yet because you don't fall within that spectrum for a medical doctor to diagnose you, we can still catch it. If you have full-blown Hashimoto's, fibromyalgia, or lupus (I've treated them all), then it's going to take some work, and you need to be mentally prepared for that.

Tracey Lee: Prevention, prevention, prevention. I think when we keep on this path, this is where it's going to go. That could kind of branch off to these different areas. It may not just be just this. And those consequences could be like different types of symptoms leading to different, which are a symptom of something greater, that's not good for us. So, when you do this assessment, are you able to show people that this is the direction you're headed? So you go, holy crap if I keep doing this, then I'm going to go, I'm going to go to one of these places essentially, maybe more than just one of them. Is that what you can show people when you do them?

Ariel Jarvis: Our blood work and a life machine and other machines. We have crazy technology at our clinic. We're able to determine what is coming down the pipeline for you if you're not careful. And then we would go and investigate a bit further. We would get you to get some blood work with your medical doctor to check certain things. Even if you're not in the spectrum, say it's thyroid or whatever, and you're not in the spectrum, and they say, "Oh, fine, go home," I'm going to see where you are outside of the spectrum because they only look to see if you're in the spectrum to prescribe medication. I look to see where you are on the spectrum, even if it's an outlier, for optimization. It's about thriving, not surviving.

Tracey Lee: Right, optimizing your current, like optimizing your body, which is the vessel, that's what you want to thrive. So, how do we take you from this, not plugging it with more stuff that's really been hurting you over time? Let's take your body and optimize it so those symptoms go away. So, all of a sudden, your body's repairing, and you're thriving. That is so powerful.

Ariel Jarvis: It has been debunked that when you get older, you will get these diseases and these symptoms. Oh, that's just a sign of, you know, aging, your kidneys are going, your heart is going, your joints are going. None, none, none, none, no. That's the cell blueprint. That's the recipe for disaster if you're not biohacking. You can biohack that. The way you should pass away is your heart should stop. Your heart has a certain number of beats in your lifetime, and when you're done, it stops. That's how you should go. Pain-free.

Tracey Lee: So, do you have to physically go to your location to do this?

Ariel Jarvis: No.

Tracey Lee: You can do this so anyone can tap into this. Okay, so let's talk about that because when I stepped into my calling, it was just growing and growing and growing. I know because of that growth I have to be optimizing the vessel that's showing up to do this today. I mean, if I'm feeling crappy, if I'm not sleeping, if I'm dealing with some symptoms that are underlying reasons for something else that's manifesting, I can't do what I want to do. And I either settle for that, or I don't. And for me, I don't settle for that. So, how does someone who lives not in BC near where you are, how do we get you to help us with this?

Ariel Jarvis: I have a lot of patients all around the world. You will be limited on the testing that we can do, but here's the thing. I've treated over 2,500 patients now in my career. I've seen a lot of patterns. You just start to see patterns. We will email you an intake form. I do iridology. So left eyes, everything you've genetically inherited from mom, right eyes from dad. I look at the blueprint there. It tells me everything about your 11 body systems. You'll take a picture of both eyes with your phone and email it to me with the intake form. And then if you don't have any updated blood work within the last three months, you need to go get all that done. I will help you with that. If you need a medical doctor, we will help you with that because we have a medical doctor who can help you with a requisition for whatever you need if your doctor's not cooperative. And I help anyone around the world. I have patients in Australia, Toronto, Hawaii, Ireland, Iceland, like it's crazy. So, obviously, there's a time zone change. Sometimes, I'm working on Zoom at four in the morning, just because of the time zone, right? I won't turn anyone away. But at the same time, I will vet you. And if I feel like you're not in an environment where you're ready to grow and you're ready to make those growing-pain changes, then you need to reach out when you're ready. Because it's going to take some work, especially, if you have multiple conditions.

Tracey Lee: Wow. And I think you're like me, we are very direct people because we want you to get results in your life. And until you know what it's like to have them and to not have them, you don't really know what that difference looks like, you don't have anything to compare it to. You just kind of settled for how you feel and that's it. So until you realize something different, you just settle, and you haven't settled. You just really really want to help people, and you're right, you do have to be ready, but I think what people do is that that second of readiness can be overshot by the fear of finding something out that you don't want to find out. It's really important because I've been in the wellness phase, too, for five years, educating people on ionized water and how to access it in their homes and everyday lives. I observed people avoid going deeper into their health concerns out of fear of what they may eventually find out. It's either you initiate it, or eventually, you will be forced to find out when it's at a point where now it can impact your life in a very, very negative way. Why not reclaim your power so you can create the life you want by grabbing onto some information?

And here's the thing: Understanding will render the fear useless. Because now you are equipped with information that you can at least make a decision about. You can begin to feel self-empowered about your health and life. Waiting is when the mind takes over, and fear runs your life. That is no way to live. Yet so many do. But once you know something, you can't turn it back. And that's what the summit's about. We're giving you information. We're giving you ideas that you then have a choice to make. What comes next? Ignore it, and you're ignoring yourself. And if you're ignoring yourself, where's your self-worth? Maybe that's where you want to start working. Recognizing when you say no to things you want the result it brings, it's got to do with how you feel about yourself. And if that's where you have to start the work to get ready to be with Ariel, to be supported by any of these amazing speakers, then that's where you need to get ready. And that's where you need to ask for support to do that. Right?

Ariel Jarvis: Yes. And here's the thing: It's not as hard as you think. People overcomplicate it. I've had so many patients come in where they're like, okay, am I your worst patient? And I'm like, no, and they come in and they've got a laundry list of symptoms, but it all came from one body system. We correct that one root cause, all the symptoms go away. People don't realize things are connected.

Tracey Lee: Okay. Walk us through it.

Ariel Jarvis: You could have 10 things going on. I get rid of one bad apple, and everything's back to normal, and people are just shocked. They're like, they think I'm a wizard, and I'm like, no, it's just your body is your body wizard. It's so cool. And I take something complicated in the body and I make it super simple for you to understand because my job is to empower you and help you get independent with your health. And if you can learn that your body and your cells can transform from a really bad diagnosis to optimizing your life and you being pain-free or diagnosed-free, think about what else you can biohack outside of your body, your job, your marriage, your finances, everything everything, but it has to start on a cellular level because that's what is making the actions you take in everyday life.

Tracey Lee: Wow. Okay, before we go, because stories are the best thing, right? Because it allows us to get into our imagination and start to really feel it. Can you give us a client story? Just kind of walk us as easily as possible through someone who came in, this is what was going on, this is what you did, this is how it turned out. Can you change that?

Ariel Jarvis: I have one very quickly. This lady had an addiction, she had heroin, meth, all of it. Then she decided to get clean, but all of that stayed in her cell memory. Then she had to go on all these medications because her body started to deteriorate. She was only in her 40s. And the poor diet, the poor water, all of it. She stumbles into my office. She's now been off all of the street drugs, but she's on 13 pharmaceuticals that are damaging her liver and her kidneys, and then she's taking stuff for this and then this blah, blah, blah, blah. So, long story short, because of her lifestyle choices, her skeletal system is the one that took the biggest hit. Your skeletal system is your bones. Your bones are a storage of alkaline minerals, which means the more acidic you are, the more the minerals come out of the bones to buffer the situation in the body system that's taking the hit from the acidic level. Her bone density was so brittle that her spine was starting to collapse and just dissolve. So her medical doctor had booked her surgery within six months to put a rod in her back and steel plates all in her lower pelvis. And they said she may not be able to walk again. She will be in a wheelchair. She came to me and she's like, "I don't know if you can help me." I said, "We're going to biohack you." We're going to grow back your bone density "because your cells turn over every 25 days on average." And we're going to actually test your bone density before and after.

I changed her diet. I changed her water. Then she didn't need certain medications anymore for the blood pressure, the blood thinners and the satins and this and this and this, and it just went on and on and on. We're working with her medical doctor, and her medical doctor is like, what are you doing, you don't need these four drugs anymore, and then the next month, what are you doing, you don't need these three drugs anymore in the next month. She was only on one more drug, and all 12 drugs were gone after four months from the biohacking. Her body responded so quickly, and I said I want you to get your bone density checked again. So, her specialist tested her and canceled her surgery. Her bones had grown back because of our protocol and our biohacking and the rapid growth in her testimonials on my YouTube channel, my Instagram, everything. I have tons of testimonials like this. She no longer needed that surgery. She lost 60 pounds. She quit smoking. She quit all the drugs. Her liver toxicity improved so significantly because she dialed in. She went all in, 100 % all in. She did a full reset of everything. Even the people she surrounded herself with, even the music she listened to, even the time she spent outside, everything, her job, everything. That's why she goes for a walk with her dog, and her spine is completely fine.

Tracey Lee: Oh my gosh, that's incredible, Ariel.

Ariel Jarvis: I know.

Tracey Lee: It's so inspiring. Oh my gosh, you're just amazing. And I know every time I talk to you, I'm like, I wish we lived close together. I'm just going to come and visit you in BC, and then you're going to take care of all this stuff for me. We'll just do a family thing because I want to live my best, I want to be freaking rocking it when I'm in my 80s and my 90s. I want to be the coolest freaking grandmother and be rocking it out. That's what I think we all need to tap into. And we deserve that.

Ariel Jarvis: Yes.

Tracey Lee: This is what you can do. You can help us get there. You're so amazing. Okay. I love you. I love you. I love you biohacking your way to a better life. Ariel, you're the best.

To watch Tracey Lee's interview with Ariel Jarvis, scan the QR Code below.

Melissa Trumble

Founder of ZFG Living LLC

https://www.linkedin.com/in/melissa-trumble/
https://www.facebook.com/melissa.trumble.zfg/
https://www.instagram.com/zfgliving/
https://zfgliving.com
https://calendly.com/zfgliving/zfg-living-intro-call

Melissa Trumble is a life-transforming force and the founder of ZFG Living. As a life coach, speaker, podcast host, and bestselling author, Mel's mission is empowering individuals & powerful survivors of life to make sense of the chaos & overwhelm and turn it into their superpower and unleash their authentic joy. Drawing from her journey of overcoming abuse, traumas, and limiting beliefs, Mel shares insights and wisdom with humor, candor, and a deep understanding of what it takes to live life to the fullest. Through her life coaching programs, speaking, podcast, and "The Big Book of Bad Ideas" book series, Mel leads the way for people everywhere to heal their past, challenge their limiting beliefs, and create a life of joy and authenticity.

How to Unleash Joy and Live Your Badassery

By Melissa Trumble

TRACEY & JENN MOMENTS

Jenn Iannuzzi: Did she say Liger?

Tracey Lee: I know, I don't know what that is.

Jenn Iannuzzi: Oh my God, I do.

I don't.

Jenn Iannuzzi: So, *Napoleon Dynamite* was like this epic cult movie. If you know the video, favorite animal of Pedro's or was it Napoleon's?

Tracey Lee: I love that movie. That's a ridiculous movie.

Jenn Iannuzzi: Oh, it's awesome. So, it's a cross between a lion and a tiger. Mel, if that's what you said, I love you even more.

We'll get Mel to clarify that because, yeah, Mel's friggin cool. Liger is the best. She just wrote in the comments. Oh my god. Oh my gosh, what did you do on lunch break?

Jenn Iannuzzi: Oh, for joy? Everyone was going to do something joyful. I went for a walk, and then like I said to Archer in the chat, I had to clean all this poop off Pepper's ass. So that was my lunch hour, but I also ate and went for a walk.

Tracey Lee: Yay. I went and hung out with my daughter for a bit and then my husband. My husband is an amazing chef.

Jenn Iannuzzi: Yes, yes, oh my god, you guys.

Tracey Lee: He is, right? When people come to our parties, they don't eat for a day because they know the food's going to be all fresh, all real.

So, he made me this beautiful platter with, picture this, one row of salad, then there was a row with couscous and this beautiful chicken medley. And then there were other things. I just went all in and ate it, and it was so good. And there is nothing that brings me more joy than when people make food for me.

Jenn Iannuzzi: Well, then, Herb is your joy purveyor because he's always making you delicious meals.

Tracey Lee: Always. Always. My daughter says, "You know, Daddy treats you a bit like a princess, Mom." I'm like, all right, I'll own it. I will own that when it comes to food. Yes, so that brought me joy. And I went out and shared on Instagram about all the beautiful speakers so far how and how amazing they are.

Jenn Iannuzzi: Oh, wait. What did everyone else do for joy? Write it in the comments.

Tracey Lee: Yeah, write it in the comments.

Jenn Iannuzzi: Did Herb make you a delicious lunch? Probably not, but you'll get to if you get close with Tracey, right?

Tracey Lee: If you live close to me, you can come over. I will open up my house to you. Absolutely. What brought me joy was thinking of three new ways I can support women.

Jenn Iannuzzi: Hello!

Tracey Lee: Yeah, but there are three beautiful things I'm going to be talking about, and I'm so excited. And that's above and beyond the events that I'm planning for the next few months. That's what brings me joy coming up with new ways to celebrate women like we are here and new ways to help women in our beautiful Get Out of Her Damn Way container, which you're not going to want to leave, by the way. Would you like this extended? Like extended and extended and extended? I'm just wondering because the reason why that's important is what we talked about today, Jenn. Why would that be important?

Jenn Iannuzzi: Community, accountability, and staying in the energy. So, you're making decisions for you.

That clock, right?

Jenn Iannuzzi: Yeah.

Tracey Lee: The default clock. You want to change your default clock. And the more you're in the energy of things that are going against the default, you're going to be able to change that default clock, and you're going to be able to actually do a reset, right? Do a reset, like Ariel talked about those things, right? We need to make sure we're doing all of those things that she talked about. She talked about, I don't know if you remember, I need to go into all my notes.

Jenn Iannuzzi: Are you talking about the five core values? I have them.

Tracey Lee: Well, not the five core values. I'm talking about picking your poison.

Jenn Iannuzzi: Oh, right.

Tracey Lee: Pick your poison. Not too many, and don't do them very often. So we need to choose and call it what it is. Not too often, not too many. And then she said, reset often.

Jenn Iannuzzi: Is wine a poison?

Tracey Lee: Yeah, well, it's wine. Anything that doesn't nurture you and your cells, I don't think your cells need wine.

Jenn Iannuzzi: Probably not.

Tracey Lee: No. This is about being direct, loving, and honest with ourselves. I spent much of my life in avoidance mode, refusing to face things because I didn't want to deal with them. I thought if I ignored it, it would just disappear. But that never happened. What we need to recognize is that once we decide to stop avoiding, we have to ask ourselves, "What steps can I take to reclaim my power and become less avoidant?" That's when we lean on the community we're building. This is a powerful women's circle that's only going to grow as we welcome more women into this supportive space. So, if you're watching this and feel called to join this circle, reach out to me. I'm already planning some exciting things for next year, and you'll want to be part of it. There will be opportunities to get involved sooner rather than later, and I'll keep you updated!

Tracey Lee: Okay, we have an amazing person coming in right now. I did not know this incredible being until the summit. I was fixated on a certain part of her that I'm sure you'll understand when you see her; you may have seen the picture of her.

Jenn Iannuzzi: The glasses?

Tracey Lee: Yes, those glasses are my favorite color, and she totally rocks them. Jenn, you're that kind of woman too! You and Mel in the same room would be something else. You should definitely keep those on while you introduce her. Mel has this undeniable cool factor. I don't have it, and I'm okay with that, but she definitely does. Get ready to jot down her one-liners because she always delivers some gems. I'm excited to see if she drops any today. Alright, Jenn, take it away and bring Mel on!

Introduction

Introducing Mel Trumbull, the life-transforming force behind ZFG Living LLC. Mel's mission is to empower individuals to unleash their authentic joy, drawing from her own journey of overcoming abuse, traumas, and limiting beliefs. Through her Life Coaching Programs podcast and the "Big Book of Bad Ideas" book series, Mel guides people everywhere to heal their past, challenge their limiting beliefs, and create a life of joy and authenticity.

Mel's first job was as a cashier at a deli, where she likely began honing her people skills. Her favorite month is October, and she has a special fondness for the fall season—both times of change and transformation, much like the work she does with her clients. Mel's favorite animal is a liger, a unique blend of strength and rarity, much like her own journey. Teal and aqua are her favorite colors, reflecting her vibrant and refreshing personality. When it comes to food, she's all about anything spicy, bringing a bit of heat and excitement into her life.

Her favorite word is "Moffo," and the word she despises hearing is "Cannot," reflecting her belief in possibilities and overcoming limitations. While she doesn't struggle much with pronunciation, "Supercalifragilisticexpialidocious" is one word that gives her pause.

Mel texts her husband the most, showcasing the close connection they share. She's found that her 50s are her favorite age so far, a time when she's truly embraced her authentic self and purpose. For a lazy dinner, she turns to anything frozen from Costco—a practical choice that allows her to focus her energy on more meaningful pursuits.

In the summertime, Mel loves to hike, connect with nature, and enjoy the outdoors. She's diligent about flossing a couple of times a week and shares her home with a cat, showing her softer side. While she doesn't have biological children, she is a stepmother, and she is happily married.

When asked to choose between love and friendship, Mel sees them as one and the same, reflecting her belief in deep, meaningful connections. Happiness always trumps money for her, and she values both cats and dogs, appreciating the unique qualities each brings.

The best advice Mel ever received is to "pick up your pieces and move on," a mantra that has undoubtedly guided her through life's challenges. She wishes she had learned mindset work sooner, as it's become a cornerstone of her personal and professional growth. Her deepest fear is not helping others, which drives her dedication to her mission. Mel's biggest flaw, as she sees it, is her struggle with boundaries—something many can relate to.

During the holidays, you can find Mel indulging in her favorite treat: pecan pie, a sweet reminder of the warmth and comfort she strives to bring into the lives of others. Through her work, Mel Trumbull is a beacon of hope and transformation, showing us all that it's possible to live a life filled with joy, authenticity, and boundless possibilities.

INTERVIEW

Melissa Trumble: Hello, hello. Good to be here.

Tracey Lee: Have you ever had an intro like that before, Mel?

Melissa Trumble: It's gorgeous. And quite frankly, the shades Jenn was wearing made it.

Tracey Lee: Right, she was channeling you, Mel. Okay, before we start, you need to tell everyone what ZFG means.

Melissa Trumble: ZFG is zero Fs given, Fs spelled, F*CKS. Keep it PG, baby. And what that is is your resources. And when I say ZFG, I mean don't give yourself away. Because I was raised in the Deep South, I grew up to be a shadow human just to support others, right? And I just gave all of my resources, my time, my attention, my care, you know. I set up businesses for ex-husbands as if it were my job. And once I realized the commonality, oh, when the ex-husbands became plural, I was like, oh, wait a minute, that's me. I'm the common denominator. Ah, humble pie for everyone. So, I just realized you can't give yourself away.

And then I got into understanding how to actually rewrite the talk therapy and meds, because don't worry, I've also got just a host of mental situations—ADHD, suicidal depressive, generalized anxiety disorder, you know, just a lot of, let's go with the TISM, it's all there. And when you have that, it's easy to be like, well, this is how I am, and this is how life is. The fact of it is that's a lie. Because life is everything. And it's always all around us. So if you want to focus on the craptasticness of it, guess what? Each day is going to suck, just like the day before. However, if you want to look for some joy, plant some joy bombs in your environment. Like, I'm just looking up at all these amazing paper flowers that I make. I mean, fire hazard, perhaps, and yet, gorgeous, and they make me smile. So when you can alter your environment, which if you've got thumbs, you know, come on, let's do it, just put something in that makes you happy that you're delighted to see. It can be a photograph, it can be a color. I mean, this color makes me happy. So, guess what? This will be it, you know? But yeah, ADHD, did I mention that? I don't know, seeing something, and I'm sure it was really profound. So, back to you.

Tracey Lee: Everything you say is profound. As an interviewer, I have to really not become too immersed in what you're saying because I lose myself. Just so you know, I do lose myself because you captivate me. And I think I shared this with you when we were chatting before. You captivated me when I saw you on the screen with all the other women who were looking into becoming a speaker. And you were just like, yep, doing it, doing it, doing it. And yeah, you are, you're a force, and you've got serious grit and you said you were born and raised in the South.

Melissa Trumble: Yeah.

Tracey Lee: I guess, you know, you probably ate grits. Do you eat grits in the South? I don't know.

Melissa Trumble: Heck yeah, I eat grits. You can't eat grits in Canada?

Tracey Lee: I don't think I've ever had grits before, but I need to come to the South and have some grits. So, okay, when I was thinking about you coming on today, I was like, how perfect is it that Mel is kicking off our afternoon? Unleash your joy and live your badassery. Like, did the universe line this up? This is freaking perfect. And through all your funny, you know, absolute love, all the things you share, there is like this deep, nourishing, beautiful wisdom that we can just captivate some of that into our own lives. Can we just talk a little bit about that? I know we say so many things, but we want to be able to share a story. That can help others start to step into their own story with your story. So, can you share one nugget of how you got out of your damn way and how you were able to unleash that joy and live your badassery in your own life?

Melissa Trumble: Oh, absolutely. So, for me, it started young. I was a lightning rod. I was a climber. I always wanted to get away from crowds and people and things that overstimulated me. And so in kindergarten, we were being taught what our last names were, which I was just like, my name is Melissa. What trash is this lady talking about? She's explaining very patiently, like, okay, so there's another name. So, people might say your name and then say the next thing. And I was like, oh, duh, you should have explained that. And my last name is God damn it. Because I grew up hearing, "Melissa, God damn it, get out of that tree," "Melissa, God damn it, you're covered in blood," you know, like just left and right. Because my parents, by the way, were 19 and 20 when I was born. So, don't do that. Don't do that to your kids if you can. And we can now. For the time being, anyway, thank you, GOP. But my point, and I do have one, is that when we innately understand how to laugh at ourselves because I said it, was I going to a Catholic grade school? Yes, indeed I was. Was everyone, all the children, horrified? And for me, I'm just like, oh, okay, read the room, I'm five years old. And then to understand what a goof that was and laugh your ass off, I mean, that was hilarious. Mrs. Atkinson looks stricken. She, like, all color left her face, and I was just like, "Oh, is this a heart attack? Huh, yeah, what's happening?" But it doesn't matter if you're 5 or 54. I was perhaps eating an egg flauta from Costco, so fucking good, and keto. And I have my salsa. So, I'm going to dip it. And I don't know, something was annoying me. And so I just moved my hand in a way that the whole salsa thing flew at me. And it looked like I'd been shot. I had to march downstairs and do some laundry. I've told the story 800 zillion times if folks have heard it, mae culpa, but it really did look like I was an extra on CSI or something. And the ability to not get annoyed when that kind of stuff happens, because years ago, I would have been—

Tracey Lee: That's big.

Melissa Trumble: Yes, yeah, just like, bam. I could rage, no time was needed. It was the flip side of every coin for me. And it's because of having a crummy background, you know, not being raised right, that we all know our parents didn't raise us right. Okay, well, guess what? We're now old enough to vote, so we get to pick up the pieces and figure out how we're going to put them back together and do that with love and compassion in our hearts for ourselves, for them, and for everyone because we're all just trying to give them this fucking day. No one's out here trying to waylay your carefully orchestrated plan, and if you do have a carefully orchestrated plan, please DM me because I need help in that area badly. But if you give people grace and you give yourself the grace to understand that we're all just fumbling around, like we're in the rack tumbler of humanity, just banging against each other, knocking off edges, maybe sharpening some edges and just trying to get through it. Step back and look at where you are and look around you. And see, yes, there are slithering snakes, evil and badness, despair and sadness and melancholy, and all the things. And there's also humor, helpfulness, and resourcefulness. You know, you can pick whatever level of adjective suits you. You don't have to be like, I'm a badass. And that is the energy that I inhabit. You don't have to be like that. You can be kind. You know, there's room for all of us. And there are innumerable positive ways to describe ourselves, as well as positive things to see out there in this, you know, crazy nutso world. It's always been there. There have always been the wars and the power struggles and, you know, oppression and all of the things. And that's okay.

Tracey Lee: So good, Mel, like really, really, what's hitting home for me right now is, well, I love that you said, "I'm now old enough to vote." We all need to write that down and put that on a printed t-shirt or a candle or whatever lights you up because it's so true, right? We have to stop acting like we are still that child who wasn't able to think she or he had a choice to vote. We have a choice. We know that now. And our vote is the only one that counts, I would say. Yes, all these things may happen, or yes, all these things are going on around us. We have to choose to set a lens through which we want to look at things. And it doesn't mean toxic positivity. When I think about my childhood and all this stuff and then if I really go back and look at some pictures You know, there's some beautiful moments in my childhood that I know brought me a lot of joy.

Melissa Trumble: Absolutely.

Tracey Lee: So why not focus on some of those things, too, because that's all part of the mix. There are beautiful pockets of joy in everything that we do. And I love that you share that because we just have to start focusing on seeing that instead of seeing the ugly and seeing the other. And it's not even ugly. There's no ugly, really. It's how we choose to look at it, I guess.

Melissa Trumble: It's all just energy, right? It's all just energy.

Tracey Lee: Yes.

Melissa Trumble: You know, and just like a tree doesn't know the difference between wind versus sun versus water. I'm going to use all of it. We get to use what's in our world and we also get to put stuff in our world, and the number one thing we get to do is just, please give this a whirl. It's so juicy and lovely when you're waking up, and it's that sort of dusky dawn when, whoa, am I drunk, am I sleeping, I can't move my arm.

Tracey Lee: Feel for the walls for the bathroom, you're like.

Melissa Trumble: Exactly. Exactly. Then, think about what truly lights you up. I mean, what just tickles you pink and makes you so excited whether it's french fries, it doesn't have to be profound. But what really sends you over the moon in gratitude and happiness and satisfaction and all the good stuff? And then brace yourself for how you're going to belly laugh today because that is like drugs. I mean, there's a reason I love being funny. I love twists of phrase. I naturally say things in a weird way, and so I just roll with it. It's just because of how I'm wired, and it also makes me physically feel really good. And it puts your chin up. And I mean, there's science behind it. Like, people who look up and over, that affects your outlook. It affects your health. It brings everything up to a beautiful new level of positivity and optimism just by physically putting your chin up.

Tracey Lee: Wow.

Melissa Trumble: It's wackadoo. Do it for 10 minutes, and then see how you feel. Write how you're feeling, and then do it for 10 minutes. And then you're just going to be like, mother, who knew I had that power to change the channel like that, you know.

Tracey Lee: It's so huge having these valuable little resources. I mean, I'm literally thinking, okay, I wake up in the middle of the morning and am not quite awake and channel what brings joy. What will we ask ourselves, would we just say to ourselves what brings us joy right now because we just want to start to feel that, right?

Melissa Trumble: Yeah, and it doesn't have to be complex.

Tracey Lee: You know, it can be the cozy slippers I just put my feet into that bring me joy.

Melissa Trumble: There you go. It can be a color, it can be a hug from whomever you know, and then you can get to think about that and relive it in your mind so that it is happening right now because our lizard brain doesn't know the difference. They're just going to be like, "Yahoo, joy, here's some endorphins, pow!"

Tracey Lee: Lizard brain, oh my gosh, this is so good. You have such a beautiful way of turning the page on how we are all wired to think in the morning.

Melissa Trumble: It does take effort, but it doesn't have to be hard.

Tracey Lee: Right.

Melissa Trumble: Think about the lizard brain, right? Lizard brain's looking out for, I mean, when you could die from tetanus in 10 minutes, okay, like that's when our brains were evolving. So, everything looks dangerous. Everything looks scary. Everything is negative because that would keep you alive. That's what kept your ancestors alive, leading up to who you are. Well, guess what? There are no saber tooth tigers in my neighborhood. I don't know about Canada. Y'all don't have grits. So, honestly, I have no idea what's up there. But whether it's feeling like somebody's going to laugh at us, that's just as scary to that brain as being kicked out of the tribe, which means that you would thirst and starve to death.

Tracey Lee: Right.

If you even made it to that without being eaten by some animal. And so when we say the stakes aren't that high, I mean, maybe logically, but subconsciously, the stakes are that high.

Tracey Lee: Really that high, yeah. That wall gets thicker and thicker, higher and higher, and we are just creating this little circle or box around us that's like, holy shit, where do I go now? I need someone to knock this wall down with me, and this is so insanely powerful. You shared some of these golden nuggets in different ways, but you take this really cool approach when you support a client. Using that example of fear of doing something big with my life, I really hope that all the women watching this summit are going to decide to take the first step to do something big. If you think where you are now is big, there's always bigger. When my heart stops, hopefully, that's how I die, as Ariel suggested. That's how we should all leave this world. Right now, a woman has challenges, and she's like wanting to do something and she's feeling the judgment. She's feeling the comparison mode. She's feeling all these fears. There's no saber-tooth tiger in her backyard. How do you use this blended approach and what is that blended approach to help her move through that?

Melissa Trumble: So the first thing is skills. When we do feel overwhelmed, or we feel we're not worth whatever that juicy life is that we're wishing for or that we are good enough for, whatever that means, why do we do that to ourselves? But the first thing, you must get some breathwork skills so that you can reset that limbic system and get out of it, whether it's anxiety or panic or fight, flight, or freeze. And just so that you can be like, okay, now I'm here, I have thoughts, I have feelings. They do not run the show. They are in my control. And then when you can physically get that cortisol, hideous hormone, leveled out and get some calm, then you can think. Because when you're activated emotionally, I mean, I'm not making my best choices, come on. But that's why when we're in love with someone, we do such dumb stuff because we're just overwhelmed with emotion. And in the meantime, we can't remember how to count or whatever needs to happen so we have a reasonable way.

Tracey Lee: Oh my God, I never thought about it like that. That's amazing.

Melissa Trumble: And that's also an addiction. *The Female Brain* by Luanne Brizendine, I'm probably butchering how you say her name, talks about that. We get this potent cocktail, and it just overrides everything. So the trick is to find out what works for you to press pause, take a moment, and recognize that you have emotions. You're not one with them. You know, there's a lovely saying about feelings coming upon us. And so the feeling is the feeling, and it comes upon us, and we can experience it, and we can observe ourselves experiencing it, and we can love ourselves the whole time. If you're having trouble having an open heart to some things that you're feeling or, you know, being triggered by, and you're maybe angry with yourself, or we can be really, really hard on ourselves, right? Think of your sweetie pie little kid self as young as you can remember and let's really hug and love and be so brave with that little kid until she knows that whatever she feels and however she thinks, it's okay. She still has love. And once you get in the habit of going to that place, man, integration is not far behind.

Tracey Lee: That feels like an instant joy to me.

Melissa Trumble: Yeah, joy is always around us. It's just like that lovely Cherokee fable about there being two wolves. You know, one is love, all the good stuff, and the other one is fear and hate, all the bad stuff. So which one is going to thrive? The one you feed, man, the one you feed. And we feed our minds all the time with everything we see, with all whatever you're looking at on your phone, whatever you're hearing if there's, you know, some big heavy truck that goes by and it's like jarring. All of these things go in, and we get to focus on what we want to focus on (I'm extremely sensitive to noise). I walked to the library this morning, and some fool was backing through a parking lot with this big truck. It freaked me out. Well, I got to practice box breathing, that's one of the breathing exercises that's my go-to. It's when you breathe in for a slow four seconds, hold it for four, release for four, and hold for four. You do that two or three times, just keep doing it until it resets.

Tracey Lee: Your breath is good medicine.

Melissa Trumble: That was huge medicine.

Tracey Lee: I do breathwork in a salt cave. It's pretty and cool. A big salt cave.

Melissa Trumble: Oh, that's awesome.

Tracey Lee: Lying on a bed of salt. Yeah, it's crazy.

Melissa Trumble: What does that do to your skin? I have so many questions.

Tracey Lee: So, I'm on a yoga mat on the salt. Yes, but you're walking on a big Himalayan salt floor. There's a waterfall in it. It's so beautiful. I get very impacted by smells and noises. It was interesting in Rapid Fire a lot of women said they loved classical music. I asked them their favorite genre of music because some of them had that question and a lot of them said classical music. I wonder if all of these things have an energy to them, so that must be your energy that makes you go.

Melissa Trumble: I was going to say that classical music also has tempo changes so that you can't get into that sort of robotic rhythm of modern music because it just is changing. And that's just fun, it's kind of like balancing on one leg. It just keeps you agile and it keeps you going. I mean, having said that, do I listen to classical music? You know, I like swing dancing.

Tracey Lee: Sure, right? But I mean, I guess we kind of need to have our joy bucket. You can reach in and grab it when you need it. Let's talk about how we can bring more joy into our lives.

Melissa Trumble: Be intentional about it.

Tracey Lee: Be intentional, okay.

Melissa Trumble: I mean, you have to really see the person that isn't scowling and grinding their teeth, you know, whatever your stress go-to is. I used to grind my teeth so badly, I almost broke one in half. I've always been such a well-adjusted person. But when you figure out, like, hang on a second, I just had a really great day. Huh, I bet I could string some of these together. Oh, I am in charge of this shenanigan within reason, right? I still have bad wiring, but we can choose how to turn what we are looking at. What are we taking in? Are we watching grisly, scary, suspenseful things that make our hearts race and get us all amped up and get the cortisol rolling? Or does that actually release endorphins for us? Because we have such an amazing ability to solve the crime. You know, there are just different things, and there's no one way for anyone. If we could stop thinking that there's a right way to do living. That's the biggest pack of lies ever. There isn't. Don't hurt others. And let's back that up. Don't hurt yourself.

Tracey Lee: Yes. Oh gosh, so good.

Melissa Trumble: I'm not going to reverberate in fear and anxiety because I use the wrong word or something while I'm speaking. I'd never come to do anything else. We'll shelve that, I have to go do my podcast episode or, you know, busy works for some people, being works for others. That's why you mentioned how I use a lot of methods and modalities because different people respond to different things at different times and for different topics. If someone's grown up being sexually abused, then I'm not going to use a lot of romantic imagery until I find out what their jam is because I've lived that, this muck sucks. And you have to put yourself back together in a way that allows you to see the positive aspects of it because for years, decades, every time I saw an adult with a kid, I was just like, oh, yeah, immediately. And I do think a lot more kids are abused in that way than we think, just anecdotally from talking to people and having so many people say, you know, I never told anybody this. Instead of focusing on that and bringing me down, I get to focus on the fact that I can help these people because I am very candid, whether it's in my books or, when I'm speaking or when I'm having individual DMs and conversations with people. It's not a contest. And there's always somebody who had it way worse and you might feel doing better than you have the person who's, you know, doing, oh, oh, Mel, you're doing so great. And I'm just like, really? (laughing) You know what I mean? I was like that, yeah.

Tracey Lee: I love that, I love that. There really isn't just one way. And I think that we step into whatever we want to do next. Maybe we want to become a coach in this way, or maybe we want to become a doctor, or maybe we want to step into just anything that we're following our joy in. We think that there's only one way to do it. There's our way to do it, and our way is unique.

Melissa Trumble: That's weird, I can't relate at all, Tracey. That's just so foreign to me.

Tracey Lee: I think everybody has a little bit of ADHD in them somewhere, I think that that is just a normal thing.

Melissa Trumble: Things fly away.

Tracey Lee: You can just focus, and things fly away. But the uniqueness in each of us is what we have to start embodying and looking for the joy in life, and if you're not finding it then say, okay, I don't feel joyful today. Do I want to hold on to that, or do I want to let that shit go and use some things? It always comes back to reconnecting with self, right? I mean, even putting your hand on your heart could just make you remember you're actually here, you got this, right?

And you're on the right track with movement.

Tracey Lee: Yeah.

Melissa Trumble: Because when we move, whether it's just going from side to side, stomping around a little bit, rolling our shoulders, anything like that will aid us. I call it jagged energy, you know, when we just can't settle into ourselves. So, okay, give yourself 10 push-ups, take a walk, drink some water, you know? Say a prayer, however it is that you do that, whether it's standing in nature, actually with words, focusing on someone that you love, and you want to help and just send them energy, it's free.

Tracey Lee: It's free, yeah. I find the most joyful thing for me is reframing. Sometimes, there'll be someone that maybe I didn't like how they sent me a message or something in that instant. And then I go back and reread it over again, I read it from a different set of lenses. I'm like, oh, why did I think that they were saying that? That's where my head was at at the time when I read it. And I'm like, well shit. I send them back a beautiful message, and I feel this rush of happiness and joy flood my whole body.

Melissa Trumble: If we could please all stop assigning reasons for why people do their dumb assery. There doesn't have to be a reason. They could have gotten lukewarm coffee or tea and just be in a Grinch mode. Everybody's got something going on.

Tracey Lee: Yeah.

Melissa Trumble: It's not about us.

Tracey Lee: No, it's not about you at all. They're not even thinking about you. They're just doing what they're doing at that moment, right? Hopefully, it's a response and not a reaction. But sometimes we get caught up in reaction, and we go back. You know, you screw up. Move on. Fix it up, clean up your mess if you need to. Or just learn from that and don't do it again, right? And I'm hoping that women are realizing. The mess is done, it's time for you to move on from the mess and just start to step into what's next and know that you're amazing just how you are. When you've got people in your corner who can help you navigate this newness, this new idea of what you want, that's what we all need. We all need someone in our corner, Mel. Like the most successful people, they've got loads and loads of people in their corner. But they didn't get that handed to them on a silver platter. They had to find it.

Melissa Trumble: Create it.

Tracey Lee: Potentially, they created it.

Melissa Trumble: Yeah, and we can create that for ourselves. We can surround ourselves with people who are where we want to be. We don't have to already have everything figured out to get associated with people who are doing whatever it is that we want. And we also get to say, I forgive myself instead of I'm sorry.

Tracey Lee: At the end of every day, I forgive myself for all of the remote times I fell from grace today. You know, I do, I show myself love and compassion at the end of the day, and I say, I'll see the new you tomorrow.

Melissa Trumble: Exactly. And we're all bumbling around. For the four people on the planet that have it figured out good for them, number one, and recognize that they're the outliers. That's some fringe of the bell curve action right there. You know, everyone's in the middle and then there's like four people here and four people there. And they're like the ones who have nothing figured out and then the ones who have everything figured out.

Tracey Lee: Yeah.

Melissa Trumble: It's all okay.

Tracey Lee: It is all okay.

Melissa Trumble: We are just all together in the middle. And whether that's how you feel about yourself, you know, and struggling with feelings of being worthwhile, being worthy of love, and having big dreams or having any dreams or taking control over something. Just because something is scary doesn't mean it's wrong. And that's confusing for people who have their PhD in trauma, you know, because my stomach would turn over anything, like, do you want ice in your water? Oh my god, I was just perpetually in a state of panic. And so to be able to release that, and to figure out how to physically get this machine, this gorgeous bag of electrolytes and water and lightning and all the things to serve us. We can do that. We can absolutely take control of the ship.

Tracey Lee: Yeah, I love it. I love it. You're amazing. Whoo! So many amazing moments. I have just so many things. I just can't wait to see where all of this takes you and me. I feel like, yeah, the stage is calling your name like you need to have your own. I don't want to call it a comedy show, but you have a comedic space in your heart that allows people to feel like they can do it because they can laugh at themselves throughout the process. And that is a really important thing.

Melissa Trumble: And laughter. I do use it with my clients, too, because if you're laughing, you disarm the defense mechanism that's going to put the wall up. Then some of it just comes in and, "Oh, I made a breakthrough."

Tracey Lee: Woo-hoo! You're amazing, Mel. I freaking love you. I'm so glad that you said yes to this summit. You're one of the first women. I appreciate you. I'm thankful. You're awesome.

Melissa Trumble: Absolutely, Tracey. Right back at you. Thank you for putting this gorgeous thing together.

To watch Tracey Lee's interview with Melissa Trumble, scan the QR Code below.

Sandra Mercer

Founder and CEO of QueenagerVIP Inc.

https://www.linkedin.com/in/queenagervip/
https://www.facebook.com/QueenagerVIP
https://www.instagram.com/queenagervip/
https://queenagervip.com/

Sandra Mercer, a Midlife Mindset Guide, has a powerful story to share. With a background in Child and Youth Work, Sandra realized she was disenchanted with the public sector, and turned her skills towards the private sector and Customer Service.

Over the course of two decades, Sandra excelled in delivering service through management roles while raising her two wonderful boys. Now, she has embarked on a mission to help women embrace their midlife chapters, savoring every moment to its fullest potential. Sandra empowers women to reclaim their inner Queenagers and embarks on an exclusive celebration of this new chapter.

Through QueenagerVIP, Sandra has designed a range of inspiring programs that are not only educational but also enjoyable and personally transformative. From wellness tips to gourmet experiences, every woman is celebrated. Sandra invites you to join her on this adventure, proving that midlife is a time of profound transformation and empowerment.

The Midlife Metamorphosis: Birth of a Queenager

By Sandra Mercer

TRACEY & JENN MOMENTS

Tracey Lee: How are you, Jenn? How are you feeling?

Jenn Iannuzzi: I'm feeling great. Mel was amazing. Some vulnerable moments were shared in the Zoom, which was lovely. And I'm just inspired. I'm just agitated, you know? Agitated can be a good and bad word altogether. It's even something that shakes you up.

Like your foundation is being shaken a little bit, and you need to reset?

Jenn Iannuzzi: I'm having a hard time finding my footing. How do you explain that feeling? I guess you're a little bit off-kilter.

Tracey Lee: A lot of times, we can be shaken by things that were unexpected and not necessarily in a great way, and we're forced to reset ourselves. So, we're actually stepping into a world where we're allowing ourselves to go into that space where we're being shaken up a little bit. We're being supported in the reset process by knowing that we have all these women who are available to us to support us. That's a really beautiful place to be. It's being reminded. We are only shaken up when we don't think someone's going to catch us, someone's going to be there for us.

Jenn Iannuzzi: You said earlier, like this big circle of support women, it just feels like a big hug.

Tracey Lee: Yeah, a big warm hug.

Jenn Iannuzzi: Can you imagine if you went away and spent a week in this environment in nature? Can you imagine what that would be like? I think that's really where the power in all this lies. You mentioned it earlier. I mean not that you don't gain anything from being here, but unless you take action as a result of the transformation in your mindset, then you've only gone halfway. You said it's not only that you've gone halfway, you've kind of taken a step back, right?

Tracey Lee: One of the biggest things I noticed about women is we have a hidden inner glass ceiling. We will get a taste of success, and things are going well and then we limit ourselves to go further. People are telling us how awesome everything is and we create our comfort zone again. Going all the way is to keep breaking through that glass ceiling. And that requires people, mentors, and environments that challenge us. Just like this summit is challenging our perspective and how we think. It shakes things up a little. And that is so good. I have a mentor who basically gives me a left hook regularly, and I actually pay a lot for that shit.

Jenn Iannuzzi: Like cold plunges?

Tracey Lee: You're too funny, Jenn. Yes, cold plunges definitely shake you up, especially the first time. It's unexpected. You remember. I was there with you in all your bravery. Without these shake-up moments, we aren't calling upon our highest self to guide us and to leverage our inner wisdom and power.

This week, we've been sharing real stories of how these women harnessed that energy and are putting good out into the world to create that ripple effect. It is so amazing.

Jenn Iannuzzi: Mel also said some really great words that I had to write them all down. So many. She said, juicy life. She said, craptastic. She said, joy bombs. She said, wackadoo. She said, "It muck sucks," and she said, "dumbassery."

Tracey Lee: So many. That's a good one. She didn't say it today—the blame bus. Get off the blame bus.

Jenn Iannuzzi: That's a good one.

Tracey Lee: Just like wambulance, right?

Jenn Iannuzzi: Yes, that was from yesterday. I'm not just saying that to have a good laugh, and I'll be laughing about that for a while, but language really matters. The way we deliver information, I won't forget a lot of her messaging because of how she delivered it.

Tracey Lee: And I think a big thing that Mel shared that was important was there isn't just one way to achieve our goals. There's not one way to heal. There's not one way to step into what's next for us. There are many, many ways. That can feel overwhelming knowing that, but the reality is to take that and look at it from a place of, okay, if there are multiple ways for me to do something, then let go of the fear of I have to do it that way to get it. No, that's not how it works. You'll learn your way along the way. That's actually how it works. Every time you gain a new understanding of who you are and the more clarity you have of who you are, it helps you to navigate that journey and be able to definitively say what's right for you and what isn't. But when we're in that kind of messy space, when we're not feeling grounded, it's the hardest, but that's why you need people in your corner, people who really are going to challenge and stretch you because they believe in you more than you believe in yourself. They're moving you to challenge yourself to become better, more of what you are capable of.

All right, we have an amazing woman coming up. She may be wearing something on her head that might be just like, what? I love this woman so much. She's been working with me for a few months now. She's fabulous. I can't wait for you all to meet her. Bring her in for me, Jenn.

Introduction

Meet Sandra Bruce, the fairy godmother of midlife—a title she's embraced with grace and gusto. With a rich background in child and youth social work and over 26 years of experience in customer service, many of which were spent in leadership roles, Sandra knows how to navigate the ups and downs of life. But it was when menopause came knocking that she truly found her calling. Rather than shy away, Sandra leaned in, dedicating herself to helping other women embrace the full evolution of life with confidence.

Today, Sandra is the proud creator of QueenAger VIP, a platform where she informs, uplifts, and inspires women across the globe to reclaim their inner queen. Her mission is clear: to transform the midlife experience into a celebration where women feel empowered to live their best lives, no matter their age.

Sandra's favorite season is fall, a time of change and reflection—a fitting choice for someone who guides others through life's transitions. Her favorite color? Purple—a hue often associated with royalty and wisdom, both of which she embodies. And when it comes to food, Sandra's love for pizza reflects her down-to-earth, approachable nature.

When asked about her favorite age, Sandra confidently replies, "Fifty." It's the age where she truly came into her own, embracing who she is with pride. She's a woman who values love over friendship, happiness over money, and cats over dogs—a cat person through and through, just like her favorite animal. And when it comes to advice, the best she's ever received is simple yet profound: "God gave you two ears and one mouth. Use them accordingly."

Sandra has a few regrets, like wishing she had learned sooner not to worry about what other people think. But she's a firm believer in growth and self-awareness, acknowledging her deepest fear of failure and recognizing that her biggest flaw lies in setting boundaries.

Yet, despite these challenges, Sandra's life is filled with joy and simple pleasures. She loves cruising on a boat during the summer, indulging in her favorite holiday food—pecan pie—and she's soon to be married, a new chapter she's excited to begin.

Sandra's story is one of resilience, wisdom, and an unwavering commitment to uplifting others. As you read on, you'll discover a woman who has not only navigated the complexities of midlife but has also turned it into a vibrant, empowering journey. Get ready to be inspired by Sandra Bruce, the fairy godmother who's here to help you reclaim your crown and live life with a renewed sense of purpose and joy.

INTERVIEW

Tracey Lee: Woo! There she is!

Sandra Bruce: Hello!

Tracey Lee: She's got her crown on, she's rocking her crown, she's on her boat.

Sandra Bruce: "Living the life."

Tracey Lee: You are amazing. Oh, I feel you. You're so ready to rock. Okay, Sandra.

Sandra Bruce: Yes, honey.

Tracey Lee: Welcome, welcome, welcome.

Sandra Bruce: Thank you.

Tracey Lee: How are you feeling?

Sandra Bruce: I'm so honored to be here. I am so full of gratitude right now. I am so full of gratitude, not just to be here and to share my message with other women who are going down the midlife menopause path, but just gratitude for all the other women who have been here, who have been sharing their knowledge, their gifts, their blessings and just taking it all in. Like, I've got head-to-toe goosebumps yesterday and today and I'm just full of gratitude for you for bringing this together and bringing such amazing women to change the world.

Tracey Lee: I'm having the time of my life, and all I'm thinking is, how can I do this even better next time? That's what I'm doing. How can I elevate this experience for women? Thank you for being here. Thank you for saying yes. Thank you for all the growth that you've experienced along the way. It has been incredible and stepping up to things. It's been a journey, and you've just opened yourself up to say, okay, I'm going to do this. And that's where I want to start, QueenAger, let's talk about the birth of the concept because it's a really cool story.

Sandra Bruce: So, we have to go back to 2011, when my midlife journey started. I was approaching 40, and I had a traumatic event in my life. I'm an only child. So my cousin, who was pretty much as close to having a brother as I could be, took his life at 49, and that really just shook my world. Everything came to a screeching halt. This was a man who seemed like he had everything together and was happy-go-lucky. I had seen him just a couple of months before that, and he was planning his 50th birthday, and he kept saying, "You're going to come, right? You're going to come and celebrate with me." "Of course, I'm going to come." And to get that phone call saying he's gone, I mean, all of a sudden stopped, and everything in life just became almost pedantic. Like, I started looking at things going, "What's the point? What am I doing? What's the meaning of life, as cliche as that may sound?" So, it took a little time to go through that grief and figure that out.

You know, suicide is just such a different thing than someone going through cancer, and you know that journey of something's coming. It was just so sudden and so unexpected. I started working through that and looking at what I am doing with my life. As I hit 40, I started having this voice saying there's something else. There's something else, and I didn't know what that something else was, but something was making me very unsettled in everything. I was unsettled in my career, I was unsettled in my marriage, and I was unsettled in my friendships. I was just unsettled. Fast forward to 2017. In January, I decided it was the year of decluttering with my resolution. I'm decluttering the house. There's way too much stuff in this house. I have toys from my boys when they were toddlers; they're now teenagers. The shit's got to go. So I kind of started that whole mindset of decluttering. Little did I know that the universe had a much bigger decluttering in mind. My entire life started to fall apart around me. I realized that I was done with my marriage. It had been a great marriage. We've been together for 20 years. We had two amazing kids. He's a wonderful man. I still loved him. But we weren't going on the same path and our marriage was over. I was no longer satisfied with my work. I remember sitting in my cubicle one day and saying, I'm done. Just, I'm done. I didn't know what else I was going to do. I had no clue. But I knew that staying in that cubicle and doing a Monday to Friday, 9 to 5, was not in my future. I didn't see what the future was, but that wasn't going to be it. And by August of that year, I had resigned from my career, which had been great. I really enjoyed what I did. I did a lot of traveling. I got to meet a lot of people. I enjoyed it. I had filed for a divorce. I had planned on leaving my home, but that kind of worked out in a way. But yeah, everything just fell apart.

I took time to just sit back and say, what do I want to do? It was crazy, you know, and while I was going through that, I started feeling so confused, so lost. I felt really alone. I felt like nobody else understood what I was going through. I started feeling reckless. I started feeling almost like a teenager. If you think back to when we were teenagers—

16 or 17—you can do anything. I don't care. I'm going to do what I want. Almost that rebellious attitude that was coming through, and I went down some pretty iffy paths during that time. I developed an unhealthy appreciation of whiskey and scotch. I developed a little bit of an unhealthy affliction for being more open than I really should be in a bad way. It's just all those things that we kind of do as teenagers in our trying to find ourselves, coming back to do the same thing as I was in midlife. It wasn't until I hit 50 that I really got clarity on what it was.

In between, I had a really big health scare. In 2019, I went back to work for a little while doing "what I have to do until I can do what I want to do" kind of mantra. I'm getting myself financially settled after the divorce and whatnot. And so I had this major health scare. I was a stroke away from waiting to have it literally. When I ended up in the emergency room, the ER nurse took my blood pressure, looked at the machine, and said, "Gee, that's really weird. It was working just a few minutes ago." So, she unplugged the machine, reset everything, took my blood pressure again, and looked at me and said, "Are you okay?" "Well, clearly, I'm here, so something's not okay." And what brought me to the hospital, I really can't explain. I wasn't feeling nauseous. I didn't have a pounding headache. I wasn't feverish. I wasn't having chest pains. There was just something telling me I needed to go and have this looked at. Something's not right. My blood pressure was 218 over 188. Literally, a stroke waiting to happen. How I didn't have a stroke,

I don't know other than divine intervention. But it was the voice saying, "Okay, you haven't been listening. I'm going to make you listen. I'm going to make you stop and listen to me because you need to hear what I have to say. You are done with this part of your life. You are now ready to create a new life." Went through a million different tests. One of the other women talked about phantom illnesses. I was the epitome of phantom illnesses. They were doing medical tests on me that were so obscure, looking for something that might affect one in a million people because nobody could figure out why I was going through this crisis.

Well, it turns out it wasn't really a crisis. I was metamorphosized. I thought it was a midlife crisis at the time. I thought when I was 45 and I was having all these thoughts and I thought, oh my God, I'm losing my mind. What is wrong with me? And then I had this health crisis. I thought it was a midlife crisis. And I kind of chalked a lot of it up to, oh, I'm having a midlife crisis. When I hit 50, I really started to get clarity on what was happening and what I was going through, it became more clear. I was never in crisis. I was metamorphosing. I was going from this that was my life, and now I am birthing a new life. And so QueenAger came about because of a meme of all things. I had a girlfriend who sent me this meme, and it said, menopausal women shall be called queenagers. And I went, oh, that's so funny, right? And I have a special place in my heart for Queen Elizabeth. I have mad respect for that woman, Rest in Peace. But when I started looking at what it is that I wanted to do and how I wanted to bring my experience and my journey forth and help other women on their journey. I had mentioned to my mentors that I was working with at the time about this QueenAger meme and all three of us sat there dead and went, "That's it. That's what it is. It's QueenAger." And I think it's because, you know, life is better when you go VIP, right? I love VIP, as you can tell.

Tracey Lee: That's so good. Wow.

Sandra Bruce: That's how QueenAger was born, and you know, I was thinking about this this morning as I was getting ready, and I was putting on my tiara and bling. I had a woman ask me a little while ago, "Have you always been like this, or did something happen?" And I haven't always been like this. I haven't always embraced my crown. I haven't always embraced the link. And I spent most of my life wanting to hide. I spent most of my life wanting not to be seen, not wanting the spotlight, I wanted to just go along my little merry way and just do my thing and stay small. And it wasn't until I went through this journey of midlife and metamorphosizing and birthing that I came to realize I wasn't meant to play small. I wasn't meant to be in the shadows. I was meant to embrace the crown and embrace the QueenAger that's within me, and that's within every single woman out there.

Sandra Bruce: Menopause is one of those things. Every single woman will go through menopause. Every single one. Not everyone will go through pregnancy, but every single woman will go through menopause. And I look at menopause as it's puberty in reverse, right? It goes through that hormonal upheaval in puberty, and we celebrate that. We celebrate puberty. We have sweet 16s and bat mitzvahs and it's, oh, she's a woman now. And then we get to this age, and we're going through menopause and having the same hormonal upheavals, but nobody talks about it. Nobody wants to celebrate what it is to be a woman in midlife. We all know the proverbial narrative—oh, she's passed her prime.

Tracey Lee: What a stupid thing to say, past our prime.

Sandra Bruce: We're just getting started.

Tracey Lee: Prime just keeps getting better and better and better with age, right? Like wine and like so many things. Cheese gets better with age. And then you've got to think about that. There's a theme going on there. So, embracing this new place that we're stepping into that nature calls upon us without us having any control over it. The only thing we have control over is our perspective on it. Acknowledging that what we want in our lives is going to be different than it was before. What we are, what's important to us, we really have to be just like a butterfly—let go of the old shell and step into the new. It seems cliche and all the other things, but it's not. Honestly, I've never loved a decade more than I love my fifties. I'm going to be 54 tomorrow, actually. And I love my fifties. It's been the most amazing time.

Sandra Bruce: When you asked me in the Rapid Fire, what's my favorite age? 50. Hands down. I love turning 50. It was such a pivotal year for me. And it just keeps getting better. But you're right, it's all about framing that. And there's grief that comes with metamorphosis. There's a ton of grief that comes with that. I grieved my past life very, very much for, oh, I think, probably eight months. I went into a serious depression, and I didn't know why. I had no clue why all of a sudden as I'm living my best life at 49 and living on the boat. I had gotten rid of my matrimonial home from my first husband. I was on my way to what I wanted to create in my life. And all of a sudden, I was in a pit of despair. There were days I couldn't get out of my bed because I was just so distraught. I sat with the emotions. I said, "What? What do I need to learn? What is it that's causing me to feel this way?" And it was grief. It was grief for the life that I had before. And not in a bad way. Not in a "Oh, I want my life back" because I didn't, but it was still a loss of who I was before, of the Sandra Bruce, Sandra Deere that had existed before who had a great life. From all accounts, anyone looking at me thought I had it all. I had a great career, I had kids, I had a house, I had a car. We made good money, all the things, but I needed to just breathe for the death of that, the birth of, celebrate the birth of who I am now, and just continue to grow into.

Tracey Lee: And there's an in-between stage where you haven't quite left, you have one foot in and one foot out, right? I think 17 is a really awkward age, a very strange age, right? And that in-between spot where you feel the most awkward is the most potential for you to learn and self-discover. It's so powerful because you're forced to do that to navigate it with a little more ease and flow and grace and effortless way.

Or you don't like this anymore, and you're not ready for that. You kind of attack it from a crappy place. Does that make sense?

Sandra Bruce: Absolutely, it really does. It's like a messy middle. You're on the shore here and you want to go to that shore over there, but you've got to traverse all this stuff in the middle. You know, I live on a boat, so I use a lot of nautical analogies. You have to cross this river that's got huge currents and riptides, and the waves are bashing against you, and you are trying to fight through it because you can't go back. After all, you've gotten this far. Going back is pointless because it's going to be just as hard to go back as it is to keep going forward. And the good stuff's on the other side. The grass is greener on the other side.

Tracey Lee: So, let's talk about navigating this space because I think you said we don't need to know the how, but we need to know the why. And the why can be why is this happening? And that understanding gives us the substance that we need to say, okay, now I get this. It's not because I'm a freak and I'm going crazy; it's because this is actually what my body is experiencing, but now I get to choose how I want to respond to that, and that's going to allow me to step into the next. What are some things that you help guide women like me through this metamorphosis? So we can step into our queenagerness!! How do we start this journey? Walk us through because I know you've created an amazing ebook and so many amazing things. Can you help us walk through some of that experience?

Sandra Bruce: We have to go back to that little girl. It really stems from going back to that little girl because that little girl was born for greatness. She was born to be bold, and we were all given gifts to share with the world. But here's what happened. Life happened. We came into a world where we were told, okay, well, little girls are made of sugar and spice. Little girls are nice. Little girls do this. And little girls don't do that. And as we grow up in this society of patriarchy, I'm not going to go down that road because it's a little bit cliche and it's a little bit overdone, but we live in a world where women and men have different roles. So, we grow up with this in different variations of families, obviously, and we've got other traumas that jump in there so that when we get to this midlife where things have been going along, and we've been playing the role that we've been told we have to play.

Once we hit midlife, there's something that clicks inside us. And it says that is not what you were meant to do. You are not fulfilling the role that I gave you. You need to change. And most of us will sit there and go, I don't know what you're talking about because I'm just fine. I'm running along. I've got everything I wanted. I've created the life I want, and it's not until something traumatic happens that most of us will stop and say, oh, wait a second, maybe there's something here.

What I help women do is try to avoid the massive trauma or the massive setback, be it a health issue or be it a literal falling apart. I help women try to make falling apart a little bit easier. And oftentimes, it's women who'll come to me and say, I don't know what's happening, but I think I'm losing my mind. And they don't know what their path is. Some women come, and they're already on the path. A lot of the women here, they already know they want to get out of their damn way. I know that I know that I'm on this path. I just need some help figuring out where the path is. And that's great. And we work on that. We're going to do a vision board. We're going to start creating a life. We're going to dig into it. What is it you desire? For other women, it really goes back to "what brings you joy." What lights you up every day? I've had some women where we start, so basic we go, what's your fives? Look at your five senses and tell me one thing for each sense that lights you up. What lights you up visually? When you hear that sound, what lights you up? When you smell that smell, what fills you with so much love? And we start that small.

Tracey Lee: That's really cool. Those are such simple things that we can do. That really connects us to what we like. What brings us joy? That's a really easy exercise. I love that.

Sandra Bruce: I've asked that question to so many women. What do you want?

Tracey Lee: Yeah, that's a loaded question.

Sandra Bruce: It is a loaded question because we don't know. We've never allowed ourselves to dream. We don't allow ourselves to put our needs and our wants first. Forget about needs. What we want front and center.

Tracey Lee: That moment, right? That "I'm not meant to do this" moment. That's the moment when I really embodied why I'm here. But there was that moment where I had to walk away from a business that I had been growing for four years because I just knew I wasn't meant to do that anymore. If you work so hard and you've done so well, you've been successful and you have a team and all this, I'm like, yeah, but I'm not meant to do that. I know I'm not meant to do that inside my body. I remember crying and going, how can I do this? But I won't be happy if I stay there. Shit, I won't, that was the absolute, I will not be happy if I stay there. So, I had to have that come-to-Jesus moment and go, okay, Tracey, this is it. Big decision. What are you going to do? And I made a big decision and thank the Lord I did. That's when everything opened up. But it's having those come-to-Jesus moments. I know you use different tools to help women with that, too. One of them is helping them through that space of not knowing exactly what they want, asking powerful questions like you just said, simple questions, and then using another cool tool, don't you?

Sandra Bruce: I do. I do. I love doing vision boarding with women. Vision boarding, you know, is not what we think of getting together with the girls and a bottle of wine. We're going to do this nice collage.

No, no, no. That's not the vision boarding that we do. The vision boarding that we do is we connect to emotion and we say, what is it we want to feel and translate that into an image. Maybe you want a big house. So we find a picture of a house that resonates with the women. And I asked, okay, well, what is that you want in that house? What does that house represent to you? Does it represent freedom? Does it represent love? Does it represent generosity? What does it represent to you? And when we start connecting the emotion to the image, it just becomes so much more powerful. The whole journey of developing that vision board takes them down that path of what is it that you want? Why do you want it? What do you want to feel? Because it's all about feeling, right? We've disconnected from our feelings so much.

Tracey Lee: Yeah, and you create a space for women to give themselves permission to just literally think about their lives. I mean you can even make it that simple. I'm permitting you right now to think about you permitting yourself and I'm creating a space for you to just think about your life. I don't want to think about my life. Well, if that's what you're feeling, then ask yourself why you're saying that because if you love your life, you only want to think about your life.

Sandra Bruce: Exactly, exactly.

Tracey Lee: So that's really beautiful. So much juiciness there, honestly. You know, your story's amazing. I just learned something about your story today that I didn't know. And it tied the pieces together for me as to why you created this QueenAger movement. I know that you're helping so many women and you're very authentic. You just have this beautiful way about you, Sandra, that just lets people not feel like they have to show up any different than who they are in that moment. You're going to guide them in your beautiful way to help them unveil what their queen age or experience in life gets to be like. Knowing your QueenAger experience is just another experience because after that there's another one, right?

Sandra Bruce: Exactly, after that, you move on with the women here to help you soar through your 60s. It's so amazing.

Tracey Lee: We have this amazing circle. We got you here and then you can go here and you can go on across over this place. This is what this space is all about. This space is, I believe, what women have been looking for for a long time, all in one beautiful labor of love and support. And knowing that it's like, when you go to a doctor's office, you go to somewhere where people are doing their own specialties, but there's a beautiful aura and energy around because everyone works together in harmony. Everyone supports each other. And that is what is really important, right? And I know that you are part of that harmony. I'm so grateful for you. You're just a fabulous human being, a beautiful spirit. You're doing such amazing things. And if you want to check out this powerful woman, Sandra Bruce, know she's got your back.

Sandra Bruce: I sure do. I'll hold your hand.

Tracey Lee: Love you, Bella.

Sandra Bruce: I love you too.

To watch Tracey Lee's interview with Sandra Bruce, scan the QR Code below.

Cheryl L Greenfield

Empowered by Trauma dba Cheryl Greenfield
Empowerment Mindset Coach

https://www.linkedin.com/CherylGreenfield
https://www.facebook.com/profile.php?id=100069038382644
https://instagram.com/cheryl_g_mindset_coach
https://Empoweredbytrauma.now.site
https://winwinwomen.tv/show/empowered-by-trauma

As an Empowerment Mindset Coach, Cheryl Greenfield specializes in transforming lives through the power of thought. With over 40 years of experience, She has helped countless individuals by her mission to inspire, nurture and heal the broken human spirit by putting the pieces back together – One person-one trauma-one thought at a time. Her approach is rooted in authentic understanding and compassion. Recognizing the unique and intricate nature of each person's trauma experience, she crafts tailored strategies to guide her clients from a place of vulnerability to empowerment Cheryl's work philosophy centers on: while trauma may be a part of one's story, it doesn't define the entirety of their life narrative.

She is a published author "Becoming Me" which encapsulates her innovative approach, offering readers practical strategies to reshape their thinking and unlock their personal power. Cheryl is also a sought-after speaker known for her engaging and transformative presentations.

Trust, Rise and Thrive: A Path to Resilience, Healing and Empowerment

By Cheryl L Greenfield

TRACEY & JENN MOMENTS

Jenn Iannuzzi: Welcome, welcome, welcome to day three of the Get Out of Her Damn Way Summit. Please tell me I'm not muted. Am I muted? I'm not muted, yay! (laughing) Hosted by Tracey Lee Living. It might be the final day, but it's just the beginning of fanning the flame that was ignited in this beautiful community.

I'm your MC, Jenn Iannuzzi, and I'm thrilled to be here to guide you through a day of learning, inspiration, reflection, and connection. So far, we've heard from 8 incredible speakers on topics from building better habits to moving through grief and giving ourselves permission to dream, biohacking our lives, healing our relationships with money, building our queendoms, and so much more.

Let's bring in the host of Get Out of Her Damn Way, founder of the Get Out of Her Damn Way movement. My friend and our birthday girl, Tracey Lee! Woo-hoo!

Tracey Lee: Could I ask for a better way to ring in 54? Just saying. Oh my God. Oh my gosh. I am exploding with love today. I feel like I've never felt more loved in my whole life. Like, holy cow. Love was the theme yesterday. Fall in love with yourself.

Jenn Iannuzzi: Oh, Tracey, I have to do one thing before we really get into this.

Tracey Lee: What?

Jenn Iannuzzi: I have to do it. I have to sing. ♪ Happy birthday to you ♪ ♪ Happy birthday to you ♪ ♪ Happy birthday dear Tracey ♪ ♪ We love you so much ♪ ♪ Happy birthday to you ♪

Tracey Lee: Oh, I love you. Thank you. Oh my gosh. Thank you. Thank you. Thank you. Is anyone else celebrating a birthday today? Happy birthday. And this is day three. This is magnetic. I hope that whether you've been speaking on this stage or you've been watching this, you have just felt this little fire, burning desire, get stronger and stronger in your body. Because, oh my gosh, you matter, your ideas matter, your dreams matter. If we don't step up and show up for ourselves, why are we here? Are we here just to collect a paycheck, do our job, or just do all the things that are on the to-do list? Come on, we know deep inside that is not why we're here. Why are you here, Jenn?

Jenn Iannuzzi: I'm here for this incredible community that you've built, Tracey. That's why I'm here. I feel loved and supported and embraced, I mean, I've already connected with all of these women. I have all these new best friends now. You know, you talked yesterday about having an accountability partner and surrounding yourself with people who are where you want to be in life. And I feel like I got all that and so much more from this.

Tracey Lee: Yeah, absolutely. You know, I talk about mentorship. I hired my first mentor, who messaged me this morning. It was so timely. I was like, "Come on! Okay, how cool was that?" And I hired my first mentor almost four years ago and I haven't stopped. And I realized the things that really allow us to elevate who we are have to become our lifestyle. Like good habits that serve us, mindset, personal growth, and mentorship. Mentorship comes in all kinds of forms. I just signed up with someone yesterday because I like what she's doing, and she's doing something that I want to do.

Jenn Iannuzzi: I think what's so amazing about everyone, you know, is in sort of the same line of work, but everyone speaks so differently to somebody else. And I know one thing you've kind of taught me is different mentors for different seasons. How many mentors you've had, and how that's helped you. It's so fascinating.

Tracey Lee: Yes. I wouldn't be where I am right now without their guidance, support, and direction. I had to become aware of the areas that needed a fresh perspective and attention. When I work with my clients, one of the things we do together is get clear on their life pillars and where they are within them. It's like a snapshot of your life, really, and it's so powerful.

And I'm not just talking about health or money. I'm talking about something specifically unique to you. The areas of your life that really light you up and matter. We look for where the imbalances within those pillars are and then shine a light on those areas. So often, and this was me all the way, we avoid those areas that are in disharmony, hoping they will just change on their own. Sometimes guilt and shame are present which requires forgiveness before we can move forward. We were taught yesterday about our feelings about money and that may have shone a light on how some of you feel about your finances. When we face these emotions and take steps to shift, it feels so empowering. To make the shift, we want to ask things like who can I become more of, what role am I playing to support this current situation, what can I let go of, what support would be helpful for me right now, and what is something I can do.

You want to get in the habit every single week of checking in. How is your week going, and how are you feeling? This helps not get caught up in the busy. Busy is just in our head. It's a way we have set our mind to be, and it's a normal feeling. Being busy doesn't help us become better. It's like I lay in bed this morning. I was doing a meditation, and in the meditation, they asked, "What does complete freedom feel like?" Freedom for me is freedom from all the past crap. That is freedom to me because if that's gone, then I can actually step forward freely. And this is why you need a mentor. This is why you need support because this is a process. You can't see your blind spots or your patterns. We, including me, who help and do this for other women, also need someone to show us what those blindspots are. Work with people who are experts in their areas and challenge you to ask yourself those tough and introspective questions.

Jenn Iannuzzi: You were talking about earlier, "I am the expert of my own experience." And that really got me, you know, just to go back to what you were saying about having that mentor, having people who have been where you want to be. I thought that was really profound, you know.

Tracey Lee: People are going to give you advice and opinions all day long, but the reality is if they aren't doing what you want to do and if they aren't experiencing and are experts in their experience of what you want to also experience, then continue looking. Your mind is your best asset. I know we're going to talk a lot about mindset today with some incredible speakers, and you're going to be blown away. Truly, I hope that you take all of these three days as a gift to yourself.

Jenn Iannuzzi: I feel that's so deep. I really do. You know, you asked me earlier in the week why did you take three days off of work? You know, this is an investment in me. Of course, I love giving the gift of giving myself to you and this event, but I knew I would gain so much more from this. No, it really was a gift to myself. These three days are very well spent.

Tracey Lee: And you're a gift to me. Yeah, I love you too. I love all of you women. You know what, I just want to send you my love. I want to send you my belief. I believe in you so much. And I think, well, how can you believe in me, Tracey? You don't know me. You know what? I actually do know you because I'm a woman, and I crawled out from trauma, and dark places, and I just keep saying yes, keep trying new things. You know, my tagline is Try it, Love it, Live it. You've got to try stuff. You've got to step into things. You've got to experience them. Remember, you are the filter to life. So let in what you want to let in and then express what you want to express out. And have fun, right? Find joy today. I'm going to find so much joy today. I'm already so joyful.

Jenn Iannuzzi: Me too.

Tracey Lee: This has been, honestly, one of the coolest things I've ever experienced in my whole life.

Jenn Iannuzzi: Who said that yesterday? Joy bombs. I can't remember, but oh my god.

Tracey Lee: Oh, man. So good, and now we have an incredible woman coming on. I got to meet her in person. We were at a beautiful three-day retreat together. We went to dinner together and we connected. The last four months of getting to know her has been incredible. So, let's introduce Cheryl and just share her goodness and get ready, people.

Introduction

Introducing Cheryl Greenfield, a woman who has transformed her life journey from being a victim to a survivor and ultimately blossomed into a true thriver. She embodies her powerful motto—*empowered by trauma.* With over four decades of experience as a nurturing nurse, Cheryl has now transitioned her life's work into mindset empowerment coaching. She believes deeply in the magic of trust and the strength we all possess within. Cheryl is here not just to heal but to invigorate, guiding us to shed societal labels and embrace our authentic power.

Cheryl loves the hot summer weather, reflecting her warm and vibrant personality. When it comes to shopping, Target is her go-to store, offering a variety of options that match her practical and nurturing nature. She usually starts her day early, waking up at 6 a.m., a habit that likely stems from her years of dedication as a nurse.

In school, her favorite subject was health, a natural choice for someone who has spent her life caring for others. Cheryl grew up in Trenton, Ohio, a place that undoubtedly shaped her resilience and strength. When asked to name a four-letter word that starts with 'B,' Cheryl found it tricky, but her thoughtful nature shines through in every response.

Her hero is her father, a figure who likely played a significant role in her journey from victim to thriver. Cheryl's last vacation took her to Canada, a place where she probably found peace and inspiration. As a child, she was afraid of spiders, a common fear that many can relate to. Now, she's eager to learn more about crypto, always open to expanding her knowledge.

Cheryl's best dish is stuffed peppers, a comforting and hearty meal that reflects her nurturing spirit. Her favorite Disney character is Cinderella, a fitting choice for someone who has transformed her life so beautifully. When it comes to matters of the heart, Cheryl believes that the way to her heart is by looking into her eyes, emphasizing her deep connection with others.

Yoga is Cheryl's favorite way to work out, combining physical strength with mental peace. She has won painting contests, showcasing her creative side. Cheryl believes in ghosts and soulmates, reflecting her open-minded and spiritual nature. Although she doesn't enjoy running, she makes an exception when it comes to tennis, a sport she likely enjoys for its blend of strategy and physical activity.

Would her 12-year-old self think she's cool? Cheryl believes so, and it's easy to see why—she's strong, compassionate, and inspiring. She prefers to shower in the mornings, aligning with her early start to the day. Given the choice, Cheryl would rather fly than have super strength, valuing the freedom and perspective that flight offers.

Cheryl is a summer person, preferring the warmth and energy of the season. She enjoys the morning over the evening, starting her day with purpose and positivity. When it comes to flavors, it depends on the day—sometimes she craves salty, other times sweet. But one thing remains constant: Cheryl wants her loved ones to remember her for loving fiercely, a testament to the depth and intensity of her care for others. Cheryl Greenfield is a beacon of resilience, love, and empowerment, guiding others to embrace their authentic selves and thrive.

INTERVIEW

Tracey Lee: There she is! Woo! Oh, Cheryl! How are you feeling?

Cheryl Greenfield: Amazing, pumped for this opportunity. Oh my gosh, I almost have no words for the last two days. It's just so emotional and amazing women here. Tons of nuggets, nugget after nugget in this beautiful platform that you've put together, Tracey. I just love it.

Tracey Lee: This is just the beginning. This has been needed. And this is a place for women to feel safe and feel like they can share and feel a part of a community. Because not only for the people we're speaking to but for you guys as speakers, this community is very important.

Cheryl Greenfield: Yes. Yes. Right, and I just love all of the camaraderie here and how we've just built this community of like-minded people, and we can hold each other accountable. And even though we all kind of do similar things, it's different. Oh, and supporting each other in this environment. It's so needed in this world—women supporting women.

Tracey Lee: You're so needed. You are just incredible. You know, we met at a beautiful event, and you were sitting at a different table. And I remember when you got up and shared some things, I was like, oh, I need to get to know her, and said to myself, "She has a really strong message inside of her." I think you did some big self-discovery over that weekend we were together. And then you just took it and took charge, and you went forward. And I'm just so proud of you because what you have experienced and what you're doing with your experiences to help others is really profound.

Honestly, I don't know what the percentage is, but with women that I connect with, every single one has some pretty big trauma in their lives that they've been working through. You are an expert in your field, Cheryl. I just want you to share with our beautiful community about your incredible business. It's about thriving and trusting and rising up, how powerful are those three words? They're powerful, so share what birthed all of this. What birthed your business, your message, and your getting out there and making a difference in the world?

Cheryl Greenfield: Well, it started 50 years ago, this year. This past summer, it would have been 50 years ago when I got my first babysitting job, and I was so excited about that. My mom didn't think I could handle it, I think, because she was like, "Now you're taking care of children." You have to listen to the adults. You have to do exactly what the adults tell you to do. I left very excited, and I went and babysat, but my uncle brought me home. He stopped the car before he got home, and he said to me, "Now, this is the next part of the babysitting, where you get the guy ready for his wife." And I was like, wait, what? Because I didn't know anything about this. I was very naive, so you have to understand my parents hadn't talked to me about sex or anything like that. He said, "Yeah, you help the guy get ready for his wife, and you get extra money for that." Before I could say anything, his hand was down my shirt, and, you know, things were going on. I jumped out of the car, and I ran into the house, and my mom was like, "Did you do everything they told you to do?" I just said yes and went to my room. I sat there, and I thought, gosh, is this what this is about? Maybe mom didn't want to tell me because she kept saying, do everything they tell you to do. And it turned into this sort of weird loop where they would call and let me babysit. I didn't want to babysit, but my mom said, "They said you did a good job. You have to go babysit." So, it turned into I had to go babysit. And, of course, that went on and on and on.

Eventually, I asked some friends at school. I got brave enough and asked my friends, do you do the thing like getting the guy ready for his wife after babysitting? And they were like, what? And I knew right then this was not right. That's when it shifted when I went back to him and said, this isn't right, we're not going to do this. I'm not babysitting. And he goes, "Oh, you're babysitting." Oh, and then it shifted into threatening from there on out. And so for a good five years, it was in threatening mode all the time, manipulation and threatening. He would just call my mom directly and she said, "Yes, you're going to babysit." So, it was a six-year ordeal off and on that happened to me from age 12 to 18, threatening me into silence. I even tried to tell my aunt once, and he came behind me, and he's like, "Why would you say something like that?" And then she was like, "Why would you say something like that? We're going to talk to your parents if you keep talking like this." She wasn't going to believe it. He was a very prominent person in our city. So, he convinced me no one was going to believe me. And so that shut that down completely.

The sexual trauma stopped when I went to college at 18. But the manipulation and the threatening did not, that carried on for a lifetime. Threatening that he would kill me and my family, if I ever told. At all family events, he would make sure to catch me alone and remind me of that over and over and over. He even came in 2018 when my mom was dying in hospice in support of me. But when I went outside, he was right behind me, grabbing my elbow and leaning into my ear, "No deathbed confessions here." So that's how long this manipulation went on.

To survive, I tried lots of things. I did all the wrong things in the beginning, especially in my 20s, you know. I did alcohol, I did drugs, I tried to kill myself, and I ended up at an ER. And thank goodness I didn't die because I would have missed a lot in life. At that time, I met a counselor who just told me to kind of put it on the shelf: Put it in a box, stick it up on a shelf, and just don't deal with it. I did that and that really wasn't a good way to deal with it because I just stuffed it down. I can tell you that I had a complete hysterectomy at 22. I had endometriosis, and they went in again. It was my fifth surgery that year, and I came out with a complete hysterectomy because they found cancer cells.

At the time, I didn't understand all of this. Now, I can look back and say I did that with my mindset. You know, I stuffed all that down. We can make ourselves sick. It's going to come out some way, right? And I just really wanted all of that part of me to be gone. There was so much trauma there. I know that now. But at that point, I just wrapped myself in a cocoon of armor, and I reinforced it with steel from the inside. I didn't let anybody in. Every relationship I had was shallow, and I had one bad relationship after another. I was divorced twice. I was married for 25 years to an angry alcoholic, and I put up with that because I didn't feel I deserved anything better than that if you will. I was able to carry on a job. I got counseling off and on throughout all of this, but it never got the inner critic out of me. I was always constantly berating myself.

But I was successful at my job as a nurse. I even volunteered to be on the sexual assault team in the ER, so I was one of the people trained to be with people who were sexually assaulted. They would only have to deal with one staff member instead of having to tell their story 14 times to different people. You know how that goes when you go to the ER, you have to tell it to the triage, the nurse, the next nurse, the doctor, and so on. So, I was even on that team, and I was able to function, but I was never happy. I lived a lifetime of unhappiness. I could put the mask on and act like the happy mom, the happy wife, a happy whatever situation, but I was not. I literally was not.

And then what happened in 2018, I got a call from my cousin, the one I babysat. She said that her daughter, who was 18, just came to her and said my cousin's father had been sexually abusing her since the age of nine. That was her daughter, his granddaughter. And I was devastated. I was just devastated because this entire time, I thought I was the island in the sea. I thought I was the only one he was keeping quiet so he could go through life. I had never seen any evidence because I watched for it, right? Is he doing this to anyone else? I watched for it, but I never saw any of it. Of course, I said, well, I'm going to stand with her. Nobody knows about this, but I'm going to stand with her and I'm coming forth, I'm going to court with her, I'm going to hold her hand through this as well. As it started coming out, it started growing and growing, and there were multiple victims.

This may sound kind of weird that I say that I was happy it came out. I was happy because I could get the monkey off my back, right? I could finally take this huge weight that I have been carrying for a lifetime and go set that down. But that's really not what happened. I came out with it, and people said horrible things to me like, "Why would you not have reported this? You must have liked it for some reason." That was my fiance at the time. And they said, "Don't you feel guilty? You could have stopped all of this." Right now, with the last count, there were 122 victims. Take that on for a kill, right? It wasn't just one person who said this to me, it was multiple people. Strangers, family, friends. It was like, wait, should I feel guilty about this? And that is when I really dove into this deep, dark hole. I was just being sunk down. I was depressed. I was an anxiety mess. I was splitting up with my fiance. Life was just crumbling, basically. And one day, I stood on the threshold of suicide. I considered doing it again.

So that is when I knew I needed help. I found mindset work. I found a program called One Thought Away, and I thought, is it that simple? I met and hired the coach. And three years later, I have been able to totally and completely transform my life. And I can tell you now that I have pure joy and happiness. I was able to transition all of this by doing this work.

And that's my story. I know there were so many women out there at that conference. Before it was over, I had five people come to me and tell me their story that they had never told anyone. I do this every day, people come to me. I've never told the statistics, but 78 percent of women right now have had some sort of sexual trauma. I totally debunk that. I think it's more in the 90s because there are so many who've not told anyone.

Tracey Lee: And the impact of that could have been, basically, your life's over.

Cheryl Greenfield: Yeah.

Tracey Lee: Unless you're able to move through it.

Cheryl Greenfield: Yes, yes. If you're coming from that lens, all the time withholding those secrets and trauma, life is just not going to be good. I'm here to tell people you don't have to stay in that lens. You don't even have to tell anyone you could do this work. If you're not able to get out onto a platform like this and tell people about it, that's okay. But you could still do the work because people are here to help you with that. And he will never silence me again. This is why I'm getting on every platform I can to talk about it. So, I can get it out to women because there is help out there. There is a program.

Tracey Lee: Wow.

Cheryl Greenfield: I know, pretty heavy for the first thing in the morning.

Tracey Lee: No, this is what this is about. I mean, we're here to impact in a beautiful way. And, you know, the stories like that, they hit us in our hearts, whether we've experienced it or not, we know women who have. We know men who have. It doesn't just stop with women, right? And we know a voice for the voiceless, right? Someone has to step into the arena and show up so other people can feel safe enough to do so.

I was watching a show on Apple TV last night called "Good Morning." It's about the Me Too movement and all kinds of things. Women are stepping in and stepping into their voices now, and women like you are giving them a safe place to do that and direction and guidance. I'm sure when you're in that, Cheryl, like you shared some of the things, you know, wanting to take your own life and being in a very self-sabotaging world every day with every part of your life. You need a big hand to pull you out of that and help you realize there's more to life than that. And wow, wow. So let's talk about that, Cheryl. How can you help women start to pull out of this mindset mess of emotions? Bring them some clarity so they can start to see that there is more to life.

Cheryl Greenfield: The first thing you need to get out of trauma is trust. You can't move forward if you don't trust someone. And I say this: Trust me because I've lived this and have been able to move through this. I have risen through this, and now I am thriving. Trust the process. Trust the program. But you have to put trust in something. And I know how hard that is, guys. I didn't trust anyone for a lifetime. The armor, big walls, like I didn't let anybody in. So that's the big thing. You have to start with trust. From there, we're going to learn about the laws of the universe and how you can utilize those laws, which is why I like them because they don't change. I like things very solid and not changing because then I can trust it. That is what made a big difference. Then we learn how to dive deep down, unwind everything in there, reframe it, start affirming it, and, eventually, reprogram your subconscious mind to change your habits. You start coming from a positive mindset, not a negative mindset. That lens starts changing; it becomes colorful and beautiful, and you can see the love and joy in life. That's what I do.

Tracey Lee: Wow. What I'm hearing from you is, and I believe this, there is nothing that we can't overcome. There's no fear, no failure, nothing. What would you say to someone right now who just doesn't believe that? Starting at square one, the idea of trusting someone just probably makes them feel physically ill. I can't even imagine what you would say to a woman who's just hearing you right now and saying, "I want to be where Cheryl is, but I just don't even know what that first step looks like," Cheryl?

Cheryl Greenfield: Trust, you have to, if you don't take that first step towards something, you're never going to change. If you're in this trauma and you're not taking that first trust step, you're never going to get out of it. But it really can happen. It just takes that first step forward.

Tracey Lee: So, I can imagine you must feel, in addition to other emotions, shame and blame.

Cheryl Greenfield: I've had that.

Tracey Lee: Maybe not even wanting to admit that this really happened. So what does that first trust step look like, though? Do I do something small that feels like I can build up a bigger trust by reaching out to a mentor? Is there something someone could just do today to help them feel a little bit of trust? Like, I'm always about the compound effect. Small things work for us to get to a bigger space where we can take a bigger step. And when you are going through something like what you've been through and what other women are experiencing, the big step isn't possible right now. They just need a small step. So when it comes to trust, what's one small step that they could take?

Cheryl Greenfield:I would go right to a mirror. If it was me in this, I would go to a mirror and I would look at myself in the eyes and say, "You've kept yourself alive till now. You've done what it takes to survive. You were a victim, and you've survived, you can do this, and you can have a different life." Tell yourself that you love yourself, and you forgive yourself for whatever it is you're carrying. You don't have to be forgiving for the trauma because that was done to you. But you can forgive yourself for blaming or for feeling shame or guilt or any of those things. I would just go to the mirror. See, I couldn't go to a mirror, and I had a yoga teacher tell me to do that. Like go to the mirror, look yourself in the eyes. It took me probably three months standing in front of a mirror to actually look in my eyes. And that would be the little step. Once you do that, then you know, okay, I can look myself in the eyes. I can tell myself I love myself. I can pick up the phone and call a mentor or coach who can help me walk through this. Because this is not something I suggest people try to walk through on their own. It's too difficult when you're unwinding this trauma and trying to look at it and break it down.

Tracey Lee: Wow, Cheryl, look what you've done. Do you look at everything now and just realize that your purpose here is just so huge?

Cheryl Greenfield: Yes. My purpose is so huge, and I can tell you I started saying that I want to speak globally about this, and I just got a global platform. I'm a TV show host now for Win Win Women Network. I was just meeting with them yesterday about speaking globally on this and I will not be quiet. There's too much of this going on in the world. Well, and even men too. I'm not counting men out in this. They don't have the resources to come to help them deal with this trauma. And yes, counseling can help you. I don't say don't go to counseling. It just didn't work for me. It was just telling my story over and over again. It didn't give me the tools I needed. I needed tools. So when my inner critic started berating me, I needed a tool to say stop this. This is how we're going to think differently.

Tracey Lee: Right. And you give them those tools. That's amazing. Your work is undeniably profound. It's undeniably needed. It's mission-critical. And you know, whether those stats are 78% or 88% or 98%, I'm on board with you. I do believe they're way up there in the 90s, which just tells us all of this work, If you don't have someone guiding you through this, your life's going to stay where it is and probably get worse. I would think if we don't spiral up, we spiral down without support.

Cheryl Greenfield: Absolutely.

Tracey Lee: Yeah, so beautiful. Oh my gosh, Cheryl. Woo, the emotions are flooding my body. I'm so grateful for you.

Cheryl Greenfield: Thank you so much, Tracey, for this platform.

To watch Tracey Lee's interview with Cheryl Greenfield, scan the QR Code below.

Debbie Calladine

Immersed Coaching & Consulting Solutions
Transformational Mindset Coach

https://www.linkedin.com/in/debbiecalladine/
https://www.facebook.com/debbie.calladine.1/
https://www.immersedcoaching.com/

We are the "Bridge," closing the "GAP" from Hell to Heaven on your journey to "Living Authentically." Transformational mindset coaching goes beyond the concept of a growth mindset, inspiring meaningful and lasting change that helps you become your best self. Our potential is limitless, and as we adapt and evolve, we continuously reshape who we are, what we do, and the life we lead to navigate a world that is constantly changing. Together, we share a vision of both the journey—'I am transforming'—and the destination—'I am transformed.'

Your Higher Self + Your Higher Goals = Your Key to Success

By Debbie Calladine

TRACEY & JENN MOMENTS

Jenn Iannuzzi: Tracey, you're muted now. I love that you had your mute moment.

Tracey Lee: I had my mute moment.

Jenn Iannuzzi: I love it, I love it, I love it.

Tracey Lee: Number two. A lot has happened since I took my break. I went and did something, and I'm like, why am I doing this? But God told me to do it. It has to do with the government and I needed to make a phone call. So I did that. And I feel really happy and proud of myself because sometimes we avoid things. We create these stories in our heads, and we're like, "Ew, I don't want to do that."

Jenn Iannuzzi: I had to make that call too, a few months ago.

Tracey Lee: Well, my call was a good one. Here's the thing: We all have things that we don't want to do.

Okay, let's jump into this. First of all, you know, Debbie is stunningly beautiful, but what I got to know about Debbie in the last year is that she has such a beautiful heart. I think I've helped her open up her heart a little bit. I'll let her decide if she thinks that's true. She's a very cool person because she says what she needs to say, but she also walks the talk. She doesn't just say the shit. She really walks the talk. She pushes herself hard. And I think she's learning to love herself a little bit more. That's why I know that this week has been really good for her.

Jenn Iannuzzi: I told you before that I can't wait to hear her speak because she has been such a supporter of everyone in the chat. She is leading that chat with all kinds of cheerleading, support, and encouragement and dropping all the golden nuggets.

Tracey Lee: Well, she also won a contest to invite the most people to the summit.

Jenn Iannuzzi: I have no doubt.

Tracey Lee: She goes all in. Can't wait for you to meet her. Introduce this badass, beautiful, bold, bodacious woman who I just adore.

Introduction

Introducing Debbie Calledine, a rising mindset coach whose journey from self-doubt to discovering the power of a resilient mindset has transformed her into a beacon of empowerment for others. Debbie didn't just overcome her challenges; she turned her experiences into a powerful toolkit designed to inspire and uplift. She's a living testament to the magic of the right mindset and the impact of mentorship.

Debbie's bed is always made, reflecting her disciplined and organized nature. If she could drive any car, it would be a red Maserati—a bold choice for a bold woman. Although she's never written a song for anyone, she's not one for crafting either. Debbie has no regrets when it comes to spending money, embracing each decision as part of her journey.

When it comes to movies, Debbie enjoys quoting *The Pursuit of Happyness*, particularly inspired by Will Smith's performance—a fitting choice for someone who values resilience and perseverance. If she could be transformed into any animal, Debbie would choose to be a tiger, embodying strength and determination. Her hero is her mom, who undoubtedly played a significant role in shaping her resilient mindset.

Debbie's last vacation took her to the vibrant city of Las Vegas, where she likely enjoyed the energy and excitement. In her free time, you'll find her working out, a testament to her commitment to both physical and mental strength. Her favorite subject in school was drama, reflecting her love for expression and storytelling.

Debbie grew up in the small town of Hepburn, Saskatchewan, and now resides in Saskatoon, Saskatchewan. Her favorite body part is her eyes, which perhaps mirror the depth and insight she offers as a coach. "Bonjour" is her favorite word in another language, a simple yet elegant expression that matches her personality. When it comes to dessert, anything with chocolate is her go-to, and for breakfast, she enjoys classic eggs and bacon.

If Debbie had to change her first name, she would find it tricky and prefer to pass on it—perhaps because she's so comfortable in her own skin. She's street smart, learning best by doing rather than just watching. When it comes to food, she prefers fresh over fried, aligning with her healthy lifestyle. Debbie is more bold than cautious, but when it comes to jumping into a pool, she'd rather dip a toe in first, showing her thoughtful approach to life.

Given the choice, Debbie would rather sleep in late than take a midday nap, valuing a good night's rest. What makes her hopeful? It's the inspiration she draws from being mentored by some of the best in the world and her passion for helping others. Debbie Calledine is a mindset coach who embodies boldness, resilience, and the power of transformation, ready to guide others toward their best selves.

INTERVIEW

Debbie Calladine: Oh my gosh, my heart is so full. I almost started crying. I was like, oh my gosh. It's so wonderful to be here with you, Tracey. Happy freaking birthday to you. A beautiful, bold, badass woman, you.

Tracey Lee: Oh boy. When we first met, I knew we were going to be friends for a long time. I think we get each other.

Debbie Calladine: You did help me open my heart. I will never forget that moment at the Alt Hotel almost a year ago. It was last October in Saskatoon at the Vision Maker, and you just looked in my eyes, and you're like, "Deb, I think you just need to surrender, you need to open your heart." I'm like, oh my gosh, is that what I need to do? I went to my hotel room that night, and I did. My hands up, I'm like, I surrender. To you God. Like, it's out of my control. I want you to just connect with my heart and show me what I need to do. And this past year has been nothing short of adversity, challenges, a lot of growth, and stepping into the woman I want to become. Can I say that that song you guys played was talking about "The Lion." I'm like, okay, I need that song.

Tracey Lee: Is it not the best song ever? When I heard it, I played it for my family, and I was singing it, and they're like, "That's the song." I'm like, "Yep, that's the song for the summit!"

Debbie Calladine: Yes, and such a great song. And today, it really resonated with me because it talked about the lion. I'm a Leo in astrology. Leo, the lion. It's funny how I said I want to be a tiger. I'm a lion and a tiger because I'm a tiger in the Chinese zodiac. So, it's kind of cool.

Tracey Lee: That is cool. You bring out the bad cats when you need to. I love it. You know, Deb, I left you that message last night about how

I see so much more beyond what you even see, but you truly have embodied the personal growth space like nobody I've ever met in my life. You live, you breathe it, you believe in it. You came from a place where personal growth doesn't exist because I spent 11 months in that industry, too. I don't know how you spent as long as you did in that space. It's just not a fun place to be, at least, it wasn't for me, maybe it was different for you. But then you stepped into this new space, and what you learned and discovered about yourself has allowed you to really really lean in and not just serve other people but serve yourself on an even higher level that's allowed you to make major shifts in your own life. Can you just kind of tell us a little of your story because the stories are so important?

Debbie Calladine: They really are and I've loved everybody's stories this week. They've been so inspiring. I said to Tracey this week's been interesting because, usually, my attitude is really good. Every single day, I wake up positive and energized. I get up early and I do the studying, I do the workouts, drink my water, and do all the things. But this week, I've been a little bit off and I have no idea why, but if it wasn't for the summit, my energy would have really dropped. So, thank you for just bringing this to all these women.

First of all, it's really helped me. And so my story, yeah, I love the quote, "Facts tell, stories sell." We've got to be willing to share stories. I was in the auto industry as a finance manager for 13 years; that was my career. I was in that career because my husband at the time thought that I would do well at it. And I did. I have so much gratitude for him leading me to that industry. But at the end of the day, I wanted to be my own boss. I didn't want to be there, you know, 50 hours a week because I had kids at home. I made really good money in that industry. I was always earning six figures. But I had to sell the products that nobody wanted to buy, right? The life disability insurance, extended warranty. So I had to get really good at selling. When I left that industry, it was very much of a man's world. I knew I was meant for something more. I always wanted to get into some form of coaching. I always said to myself, how can I be in the personal development space and get paid to do it? And I didn't know.

Here's what we got to remove the how from, right? We talked a lot about removing the how, just to really get clear on what you want. Like, what's your vision? And so when I met Dave, I don't know, six, seven years ago, we met for coffee in my city. He's like, you know, tell me about what your mind looks like. I didn't know much about the mind. I've been in the personal development space just through the network marketing company I was with. And that's how I was like, oh, I love this stuff. I love this material. And I met Dave, and he's like, what are your goals? I'm like, I don't know, I want to earn a lot. And that was all I knew at the time. He's like, no, you have to get specific about what you want because if you're not specific about what you want, how is the universe or God supposed to bring you what you want? That was like a light bulb moment. Well, I don't really know what I want. He left that impact on me six or seven years ago. Long story short, two and a half years ago, I invested in his program One Sale at A-Club because I needed to learn how to sell again. I needed to learn how to sell radio advertising, so I invested in this program. Twelve grand, put it on my credit card, didn't tell my husband. And then two weeks later, he's like, "Why don't you come to work on my team? You have a servant's heart, you have the contacting habit, and I need someone to help me grow this company." So I'm like, "Yeah, let's do it."

Like Steve Jobs says, "You can't connect the dots looking forward only back." So then I'm like, oh my gosh, I wanted to be in the personal development space. I met Dave for a reason. I invested in the program because you got to invest in yourself. I highly believe in that. And then here I am. I coach people. I sell people into the programs and then I get to coach the clients. So, it's kind of cool how it all transpired. And that's how I met you, too. And then Sven, who was not on my team at the time because he wasn't such a good salesperson. He wouldn't have probably closed you, and we would have maybe never met.

Tracey Lee: Well, I knew I was ready, though, because I had been really grinding it out, doing the work, building my wellness business, and being successful, but not at the level that I knew I could be. And I had that intelligent "ready to go, tell me what to do, I'll do it" mentality. But I wasn't given the direction that I needed. I wasn't around the right people. And that was the big catalyst for me stepping in and coming in with the mindset of I know a lot, so let's see what this is going to do for me. Very quickly realized I had to have a beginner's mindset, or I was going to screw myself royally. I had a big wake-up call, too.

I remember when I was called forward and I was told if you don't have a good attitude, this is not going to serve you. And it was all from a loving heart, meaning, you know, really wanting to see me succeed but needing to give me some hard facts and telling me what I needed to hear, not what I wanted to hear. And that was a big shift for me. I think you and I just immediately connected, too, because we are two women that show up. We show up in a big way. We also show up with a beginner's mindset. Sometimes, my ego gets the best of me. And I'm like, oh yeah, this is so great. And then I kind of go, "Whoa, dial it back, neutralize my mind, get grounded again." And that's why we need people around us who don't tell us what we want to hear but tell us what we need to hear. People who are actually doing what we aspire to do. Those are the people you want to freaking listen to.

Debbie Calladine: That direct, loving, and honest approach is key. If you're just direct and honest, you're kind of a bit of a jerk or bitch, and if you're just too loving, that ain't going to get you very far. That's how I was for many years. So you want to be direct, honest, and loving.

Those of you listening, write those words down. And stay away from people who sugarcoat the pill because they are in harmony with your paradigm.

Tracey Lee: Yeah, yeah, harmony with your paradigm. So let's talk about that for a minute because we say a lot of things. We are in this material on a regular basis. What I've learned through my coaching is being able to break things down so people can assimilate it themselves and process and go, okay, now I understand, that makes sense. A lot of the time, my biggest paradigm was you're not smart. And I've helped to understand that I'm actually very intelligent, and I do have a lot more I can work with than I thought I did. And to stand in your confidence with that, when we think about harmonizing with our paradigm, what does that exactly mean, Deb?

Debbie Calladine: You know, a paradigm is just a multitude of habits fixed in our subconscious mind. That's a keyword there. So, how is a paradigm formed? Genetically, when mom and dad had you, and then through your environment growing up that created who you are today. We all have one, and it controls 98% of what we do and our day-to-day routine throughout life. That is the paradigm, and that's what has to change for you to change your results.

You have to get really clear on what you want and then really start to do it. A big part of your paradigm, let's back up a little bit, is your self-image. And the self-image is the way you see yourself. It's your identity. How do you see yourself? Do you see yourself as not very intelligent, or you are almost like "fake it till you make it"? Step into that woman that you want to become. That's why having a goal is so important because when I first started working with Dave, my first goal was 15k a month. Dave's like, "I'll help you get there." You know, then I hit that, then I hit the 25k, then I hit the 30k, I'm going to the 40k, I'm going to the 50k a month. Some months will have a really good income, like in March and then July, I hit almost 40k, but then dropped back down to 20k. That shows me my paradigms are not set at the 40k-a-month woman, yet. So much more growth ahead of me.

It's like setting a goal. So, the 50k-a-month woman, who is she? With the self-image, you have to get really clear on who that woman is. A lot of women said this week that deep work, like changing your subconscious mind is no joke, so do not underestimate how hard that is. It is a process.

Tracey Lee: It's a really big process and it's so easy to give up because you're not getting the results as quickly as you want to. It's your results that tell you everything.

Debbie Calladine: Results don't lie.

Tracey Lee: They don't lie, and that's why having a goal, a smart, measurable goal, is important. Money is just an easy way to do that. It's important because if you can't buy in that you are that woman earning 30k, 40k, 50k a month, what does she look like? How does she act? You know, you said fixed. Fixed is the habits that we run on autopilot. And it's something that's fixed. It's so deeply rooted. And those roots are grabbing on to all the shit from your past that you've got to start to snip away at the roots to start to find freedom and reroute yourself in new beliefs. You can empower these steps into that woman who's earning 40k or 50k a month. It is no joke, but it's absolutely doable. If you can do it, I can do it.

Debbie Calladine: Absolutely. Belief is so important. It's like the knowing, believing gap, and that's huge. When I met Dave, I was one of those people that, oh, I know I've been in this information. Yeah, but what do your results say? It's like, no, I'm not where I want to be. Okay then, do you know what's holding you back? Yeah, well, it's a good question to ask ourselves. What don't we know that's holding us back? And so you've got to believe it. You've got to really step into the person that has what you want.

At the beginning, I was like, shit, I don't know, what are some of those characteristics? What do I need to start to unlearn and relearn about myself and get really clear on that? And how do we change a paradigm?

There are two ways. Repetition of thought is the only way we can change the paradigm that we have control over. The other way is an emotional impact, where something negative happens. It's death, a divorce, a car crash. We've all experienced it. All the speakers this week have experienced some sort of emotional impact. That changes us. It changes the perception of ourselves and the world we live in. But the only way we can control or change our paradigm and self-image is through repetition of thought in elite-level coaching and studying. That's the only way we have control over it.

Tracey Lee: Yeah, and that's been proven today. Women have talked about it multiple times. What really allowed them to make the shift that they needed to make, to take that first step that counted the most, was receiving help from a mentor. That's been a theme throughout this entire summit from day one. And I hope that that's resonating with people, right? Because this is not work that is possible to do on your own. If it was, everyone would be doing it. I mean, there are health books out there. You go to the library, you go to the bookstore, and there are rows and rows of a self-help book section, right?

Debbie Calladine: There's a book we study. This is a book on self-image. There's a really good resource. Dr. Maxwell Moss was a cosmetic surgeon and he discovered that we have two images. He would do work on people. Some people changed instantly. Other people didn't change at all. So that's like, oh, we have an image in the mirror. And then we have an inner image. That inner image controls everything from the way we walk, talk, and dress. Controls how much money we earn, all of it. So this is a really powerful book. But the books don't mentor you. That's the problem. If that worked, there'd be a lot more millionaires. Accountability supports the direction because you get to be around people who know more than you. You don't want to be the smartest person in the room.

An amazing book is *Think and Grow Rich*. I know several women here at the summit who have read and studied it. I highly recommend it.

Tracey Lee: It's an incredible book to be studied and study is a big part of what we do every day, you know? I mean, I've fallen off the wagon of studying the last couple of weeks to get ready for this and I made an excuse. It is what it is that now I can't go back but what I can do is step forward and continue, you know, getting back into it. And I know what studying does for me is it grounds me because this information that's available to us by powerful people who've been around for centuries, you know, it comes all the way down from people like Napoleon Hill. He was mentored by who?

Debbie Calladine: By Nightingale.

Tracey Lee: Right, Earl Nightingale, who was he mentored by? Do we know? I know Dave's mentioned that before. I can't remember who supported Earl. This is old-school thinking, but this old-school thinking is actually what we're reinventing and bringing into the world today. And we need to understand all the way back to philosophers. You know, my daughter was taking philosophy and I remember reading her work and thinking, "This is fascinating," but this is what we're actually trying to bring into our lives today. We need to start taking all of this stuff very seriously if we want to look at our age and how long we want to be around. Then think about that number of years. Do you want them to be great?

Debbie Calladine: Am I allowed to swear, like F-yeah?

Tracey Lee: Like, seriously.

Debbie Calladine: I want to say this, so you guys can write this down. This was one of your quotes that you could put in your little book. What we don't fix, our children inherit. What we don't fix, our clients inherit. So, what do you need to fix? What you need to fix is that your children don't pick up on that.

Tracey Lee: Yeah, and if you're a coach, you've got to have a coach. You've got to have multiple coaches because how are you willing to ask people to work with you if you're not receiving really good coaching yourself?

Debbie Calladine: It's true. It isn't about working hard. Working hard is part of it, but it's changing your thinking. As this book says, "Change your thinking, change your life." Right? So you have to change your conscious beliefs and habits. That's part of your thinking. That's part of the conscious-subconscious mind. It's our consciousness. That's why when I look back through my life, it's like, holy crap, I tolerated a lot of shit in my life.

Tracey Lee: Tolerated, yes.

Debbie Calladine: Oh, did I ever? I did not have the highest standards I know now. My life has completely changed. I've recently separated for two months from my husband I was with for 25 years. We split up five years ago and then got back together, and then we split up two months ago. That's been like living in my own place. That's so weird for me, it's been an adjustment, but I keep stepping into the new self-image of who I am and not going to tolerate the stuff that I did for so many years. I'm sure many of you are listening, if you're tolerating something in your life, you know deep down that something has to change, and nothing changes until you do the work.

Tracey Lee: I encourage everyone right now to take a minute and write down what you are no longer going to tolerate from this moment on.

That is one thing, but it's what happens next that matters. When we talk about the idea of decision-making, most of us are really terrible decision-makers, and we all have to accept that because if we were great decision-makers, we would be extremely successful. We're not extremely successful, we're working towards it, so the better we can make decisions, the better success we're going to have in life. There are two phases to decision-making, right, Deb? And the first is making it, but then the second is what?

Debbie Calladine: Making it again.

Tracey Lee: And actually doing what you're doing.

Debbie Calladine: I have a guy right now that says, yeah, I'm going to work with you. But he says, you know, we start today. It's like no action, no decision. So there is an entire chapter dedicated to decisions in *Think and Grow Rich*. It's not there by accident. Bob Proctor said this and Dave quotes this. He says, "If you don't make a decision within 20 seconds, you don't deserve to win." That was a bit harsh when I first heard that.

Tracey Lee: That's big. If you don't make a decision in 20 seconds, you don't deserve to win. It's like, whoa. It's harsh because it hits home. How are you triggered by that? Are you triggered by that emotionally? What are the emotions that come up? Maybe I'm angry, well, where's anger coming from suppressed emotions where you are feeling suppressed emotions like your biggest freaking champion. Go back and figure out where this shit is. The more ideas you accept that are in favor of you actually creating the life you want, the more successful you're going to be. Most of us aren't willing to receive ideas, and the most successful people have received ideas and accepted them, and that's why they're successful.

Debbie Calladine: The only difference between failures and successful people is that successful people accept ideas that you're probably currently rejecting. That's it. We're no different. You, me, Bob Proctor, anyone that's famous out there and multi-millionaires, they're accepting ideas that we're rejecting. They're changing their thinking. They're changing their standards. They're going after what they want. When we make a decision, the only prerequisite is, do I want that? If you want it, and if you want what that decision brings you, you have to do it. The money always comes.

Tracey Lee: That's good. If you want that, and then you want what that decision brings you. I like that. I like the pairing of that because it takes that to a different level for me. I want that, and I want what that decision brings me. All of a sudden, visualize what that decision is bringing you. And what does that do for us, Deb? It brings us into our imagination, right?

Debbie Calladine: Yeah, our imagination is another important faculty that we have, right? One of our six higher faculties is imagination. What do you want? That's the first step, and it shouldn't be that hard to dig into. But when you have low confidence, you have a weak imagination. So just allow yourself to dream, that's been brought up a lot this week. I cannot express that enough—dream, write it all out. How do you want to live? Partner within life. You know, like, what do you want, how do you want to earn your money? And all just get really, really clear about what you want. That's the first step in really achieving those goals.

Tracey Lee: Let's talk before we go about our higher self-image and our higher goals. I think we get confused about goals and a higher goal. So what's a goal that will help us achieve that success that we all desire so much?

Debbie Calladine: You're going to have a C-type goal. Do not set goals that you know how you can get. We set goals not to get, we set goals to grow. That's part of the self-image. When you set the goal, say, I really like to earn 50k a month because I like what that lifestyle brings me. I like that I can buy my own home, I can donate to charities, I can put my kids through school, whatever that is. I can have all of the things I desire, I can fly first class, I can buy that Louis Vuitton bag, whatever that is. Everyone's wants are different. So C-type goal, you have no idea how to get there, but that's what you want. And then the second part is creating the self-image of that higher self, who is the woman who's achieving those goals. Then, get around people who are where you want to be and watch your life change.

My life was not this way a year ago, two and a half years ago, and when I started with Dave, not even close. I'm not even close to the same woman, but I couldn't have done it without help. You're right, Tracey, we all need direction. We all need help to get to new levels. So it's the C-type goal. What do you really want? Not what do you think, but what do you want? And then creating the self-image and that takes work. That's part of my free gift is the self-image script. You start to design the woman who's living the life you want and you step into it, you record it on your phone, you listen to it, and you just burn that into the subconscious mind. There's a repetition of thought is how we change the paradigm, period. Nothing changes until you do it until you change. And that's changing the subconscious, the beliefs. That's it.

Tracey Lee: Well, the self-image script is no joke, ladies. I wrote mine in August of 2022. And I am telling you right now, that script that I still read has completely moved me into taking action, accepting new things, and embodying the woman that I am. When I wrote it, I was none of the things written. Now, I am well on my way with big plans. I've already done many of these things. I'm stepping into her, and now it's about rewriting it and taking me to the next level.

Debbie Calladine: Yeah, you come so far, Tracey. I just want to say, wow, the woman you were a year ago, Tracey has changed so much, you guys. In the way she shows up, you interview so well. You're such a good listener. You really connect with your heart so well. I'm getting better at that. But it's a process. It's opening that heart and the heart is connected to the subconscious mind. So, I just want to say congrats to you for doing the work and investing in your growth because you've invested a ton.

Tracey Lee: For sure, like literally six figures. But you know what, this is because I know I'm worth it. And this is bringing me joy. Investing in myself is bringing me joy because it's allowing me to create a life that brings me joy. So yes, there's hard work, but the hard work is the work that you will fall in love with because you realize that the other side of that work is truly what you've always been looking for.

These aren't just cliche words. When you do it with someone who can guide you and direct you like Debbie, like me, to find your people and use your voice. Finally, start asking yourself, am I willing to receive? If you're not, then that's where you want to start. Why are you not willing to receive it? There's a self-worth issue under there. And just get around new people. The best thing you can do is just get around new people. We're your people. This group is not going away. We've locked arms like we're solid. I know this circle is going to grow more powerful women who want to be a part of this to support women like you because this is what we need.

Debbie Calladine: Get in, you stay in, and you don't leave. It's like they get in and then they leave. It's like why would you leave this material every single day?

Tracey Lee: Because they haven't had a paradigm shift enough. They haven't had any shifts.

They have not had a paradigm shift yet, so you can't leave. Some people change quickly, and other people take more time. It took me about a year and a half. I'm not kidding, a good 18 months, and I'm still like, "Hey, what's the next level?"

Tracey Lee: Yep, 100%.

Debbie Calladine: I want to show people, this is a really good calendar, you guys. It's called "You Burn Me Now," so it's really good for women. And I highlighted today, it says, "We grow and learn through friction." And that's just something that stood out to me in this paragraph. Go towards discomfort, go to what scares you because that is how we grow.

Tracey Lee: Yes, I love you. You're my people. Oh my gosh. I'm introducing you to amazing people. This is what it's about. We are here to do this. I am grateful, and I just can't wait to see where we're going to be in another year. Holy cow, just look out world, here we all come together. Debbie, I love you. I love you. I love you. Thank you for being part of this amazing event. So grateful.

Debbie Calladine: Thanks for having me. So grateful for you.

To watch Tracey Lee's interview with Debbie Calladine, scan the QR Code below.

Leslie Gordon Christie

Founder of BUFFnation

https://www.linkedin.com/in/thebuffmom/
https://www.facebook.com/profile.php?id=100063601900619
https://www.instagram.com/wearebuffnation/
https://www.wearebuffnation.com/

Leslie is the creator of BUFFnation, a community that helps driven women over 40 achieve their best selves through personal development, fitness, and nutrition. With over 20 years of experience in the health and wellness industry, Leslie has trained with top figures like Bob Proctor from The Secret and motivational speaker Paul Martinelli.

As a Mindset and Weight Release Coach, Leslie excels at helping clients create visions, overcome negative beliefs, and build positive habits for a healthier lifestyle. She is a Certified Consultant with the Proctor Gallagher Institute, a Culinary Nutrition Specialist, and a Personal Trainer and Lifestyle Coach.

Leslie's unique connection to her clients comes from her personal struggles with body image during her teenage years. Her life changed when she discovered the power of fitness, mindset, and healthy eating, which boosted her self-confidence and self-esteem.

Before founding BUFFnation, Leslie was an anchor and reporter for CTV, Canada's largest private network. She also served as the associate editor of Oxygen magazine and freelanced as a health journalist for various Canadian publications.

Originally from Providence, Rhode Island, Leslie grew up in Thunder Bay, Ontario, and holds a communications degree from Carleton University. She studied journalism and fitness leadership at Humber College in Toronto.

Leslie lives in Conestogo, Ontario, with her husband Kyle, their two sons, Carter and Allister, and their Labradoodle, Ace.

Stepping Into Healthy, Fit and Vibrant ME: The Connection Between Mindset and Weight Release

By Leslie Gordon Christie

TRACEY & JENN MOMENTS

Tracey Lee: Oh my gosh, my life is still fabulous after a no. That is really profound and important for us to remember. Rejection is in our heads.

Jenn Iannuzzi: Do you know what she said on the Zoom? Nine no's until a yes. So every time you get a no, just do a big check mark and say, yes, I'm almost to the yes. She's like a master of brains.

Tracey Lee: You have to go out there and talk to a lot of strange men in the mall. To get your yes. You might get a little bit silly now, people, because our brains might be turning slightly mushy.

Jenn Iannuzzi: There needs to be wine in this.

Tracey Lee: Oh, well, that would not work, while right now I'm swimming. I've got to hold it together for these incredible women. Honestly, I'm just sitting here thinking about all this coming to an end. It's not the end, it's the first step to the next step. And that's really important for us to remember. When we think about all of this that we're learning, and we're like, oh my gosh, it's amazing, it's not about you taking it all in and completely reinventing yourself today. And I really had to get moved through that mindset because I always think big, and I want more. And my family is like, "Mom, relax." I am relaxed, but you know what? I need to relax into the next phase, not expecting the phase that's going to happen a year from now to happen quickly. Like, let go of quick, let go of fast. Let's just focus on what's one thing I can do today that I could have done yesterday. Simple.

Jenn Iannuzzi: I know you have one bad habit and one good habit, too. I think that's kind of along the same lines, isn't it?

Tracey Lee: Feed what you want to nurture. So, do you want to feed your fear, you want to feed your excuses, or do you want to feed the energy around you that brings you joy? If you want to feed that, then feed it. But what you feed, what you nurture, what you give more attention to is what's going to come more of in your world. If you're not sure about that, well, go and give it a try. Think about something that you really want. You know, I already learned about that and I test-drove it. I have a thought in my head, and it's not serving me if I don't move through that, and sometimes you have to demand it to go away and be like, that's not happening. And I told you before, I count—five, four, three, two, one (Thanks, Mel Robbins)—and it hits my prefrontal cortex, which removes the thought, and all of a sudden, you're back in the game again. I can choose to nurture the thoughts I want, and go back to the things I want, and one of the best things I do every day is write down what I want. I'll write it down right now, and I'll write it with this at the beginning. I am so happy, I am so grateful that this is done, this is done, this is done.

Jenn Iannuzzi: It's a point, isn't it? It's important to keep it in the present tense. You don't say I will be, you say I am. Is that right?

Tracey Lee: Yeah, you have to embody it like it's happened now because here's the thing: Your mind doesn't actually know the difference. We have to play in this playground of understanding we're rewiring ourselves every day if we want to.

Tracey Lee: Twice a day, I listen to Joe Dispenza, and he really helps. And it's a practice. I've been practicing this for four years. So, here's the real simplicity of it. When we talk about the book, *Think and Grow Rich* (everyone should get that book). There's a section there called "Auto Suggestion." Everything that we believe about ourselves right at this moment has been suggested into our minds by repetition. This is how we believed all the things we believe up to now. And we nurture these ideas as truth and we get more reasons that show up in our lives to affirm this truth. You will attract relationships and experiences that support what you believe, and then all of a sudden, this belief is just this ball of energy. Like attracts like. Something might happen to you in life or you wake up and you're thinking, "I don't want this anymore. I don't want this belief." So now you need to actually plant in an auto-suggestion and repetition of a new belief. And at the same time, you need to release the other one. And you have to release the other one by finding gratitude for it. It's not going to go away if you're angry at it. You need to find gratitude because the gratitude will turn it and make it less powerful in terms of how it's not supporting you. I'm grateful that that happened or I'm grateful for that experience because without it, I wouldn't have experienced this. And now I'm so blessed I'm here. You can turn anything into a beautiful moment. You really can. I mean, that might be difficult to say with some of the stories you've heard today. But I'm going to tell you it's not because these beautiful souls turned traumatic situations into something beautiful, and they moved into their power. They didn't let it hold them back, and these are the people you need and want in your corner. You need them all. And now we have the last of the speakers today.

Jenn Iannuzzi: Is that right?

Tracey Lee: Leslie and I were very new in our relationship. We got on a call and this is a woman who is in that 20-second decision-making. Yep. Bam, bam, bam. She is a freaking yes girl. She's into fitness. She does amazing things. She's got an incredible, incredible business. And I cannot wait for you guys to meet her. Leslie is another powerhouse.

She's a force. You'll feel it as soon as she starts talking. Let's bring Leslie into this gorgeous circle of ours and let her celebrate herself with all of us. Bring it in, Jenn.

Introduction

Meet Leslie, a remarkable Mindset and Weight Release Coach dedicated to rekindling the zest for life in driven women. Leslie is passionate about helping others shed old thought patterns and paving the way for resilience, abundance, and wellness. With two decades of rich experience, including her time as an anchor and reporter at CTV, Canada's largest private network, Leslie is also a certified consultant with the Proctor Gallagher Institute, a culinary nutrition specialist, and a certified Bursal trainer. Her expertise helps turn fleeting motivation into enduring transformation.

Leslie's favorite season is autumn, reflecting her appreciation for change and renewal. She loves shopping at Nordstrom, a store known for its high-quality selections. Leslie starts her day early, waking up at 5:45 a.m., setting the tone for a productive day.

In school, Leslie's favorite subject was English, which likely nurtured her strong communication skills. She grew up in Thunder Bay, a place that shaped her early years. When asked to name a four-letter word starting with 'B,' she chose "boot," a practical and versatile choice.

Her hero is her mother, a source of inspiration and strength. Leslie's most recent vacation took her to New York City, a vibrant destination full of energy and excitement. As a child, she was afraid of "everything," a sentiment many can relate to. Leslie has a keen interest in learning more about astronomy, reflecting her curiosity about the universe.

Leslie's best dish is popcorn, a simple yet satisfying treat she enjoys making. Her favorite Disney character is Ariel, symbolizing her love for adventure and transformation. To finish the phrase, "the way to my heart is," Leslie values authenticity, highlighting her appreciation for genuine connections.

For workouts, Leslie enjoys hit training, a dynamic and effective exercise method. She has won contests, showcasing her competitive spirit and achievements. Leslie believes in both ghosts and soulmates, reflecting her openness to the mystical and profound aspects of life.

Running is a favorite activity for Leslie, emphasizing her dedication to physical fitness. Whether she showers at night or in the morning, Leslie adapts to her needs. Given the choice, she would rather fly than have super strength, valuing the freedom and perspective that flight provides.

Leslie prefers summer over winter, embracing the warmth and vibrancy of the season. She is a morning person, starting her day with energy and purpose. When it comes to flavors, she leans towards salty rather than sweet. Leslie wants her loved ones to remember her as compassionate, reflecting her caring and empathetic nature.

Leslie's journey and diverse expertise make her a powerful force for transformation, helping others live their best lives with renewed zest and resilience.

INTERVIEW

Leslie Christie: Hi, everybody. How are you? Happy birthday.

Tracey Lee: Thank you.

Leslie Christie: Talk about major celebrations, right? Oh my gosh.

Tracey Lee: Seriously. How did I miss that you were a reporter?

Leslie Christie: Yes, in my past life, I was a reporter and anchor. I did it for over a decade, and actually, I was feeling very similar to what I was feeling before a live newscast as I was waiting for you guys. I'm watching the chat about the song like people are saying, oh, this song again. It was just like what used to be in the newsroom when you'd be waiting, and the producers would be talking. Anyway, what a great space. Congratulations. Are you pinching yourself or what? Like this is real. It is cool. Amazing.

Tracey Lee: Beyond. I had a vision, Leslie, and you know, I shared my vision. But truly, I had to do a lot of surrendering into the release of the expectation that the vision was there, but how it was going to unfold I didn't know. I had to let go of all my control. And as a result, all the right people came to support me. And then I had to make one bold decision after the next to execute it. And I did. Honestly, this is the first time I've ever done anything like this. From my perspective, it's been flawless.

Leslie Christie: It's a great way to go. And it's amazing.

Tracey Lee: It's fun. Wow, so cool. So cool. Okay, well, we both have a love for fitness, moving our bodies for health, and helping women feel empowered to move their bodies and to embrace their inner true beauty first, and guide them to celebrate the body that they have. To nurture it and love it and all the things.

I think that there's so much negative toxic energy around the gyms and trainers and around what we should do and what we shouldn't do. I remember women would come up to me when I was training and say things like, okay, should I work out seven days a week? Should I do double classes sometimes? Should I do cardio every day? It's really crazy that women would come in, and they would have their heads down like they were ashamed to be at the gym. They didn't think that they belonged there, they didn't think they were worthy of being there. I learned, and I know when we spoke in our first chat, that if I was to go back, a healthy mindset would be massively built into everything that I would teach. Now, thank God, there are people like you who are bridging these two worlds together in a beautiful way. And I just absolutely love it. And I love how you use the word weight release. Release, release, release. Not weight loss.

Leslie Christie: Nope, it's all emotional.

And it's funny you mentioned the gym environment and people coming up to you. I can remember just like you working in the gym, that's how I put myself through school. But I always felt it just wasn't a comfortable place and there was a lot of judgment. And it's one of the main reasons I started my business, my fitness side of my business was because I wanted to create a safe space. And then, of course, understanding the mindset piece is key.

It's interesting because the conversation you were having, the two of you before we started this is key to what we're talking about today is that subconscious program, that belief, releasing what's not serving you, forgiving it, putting some new, powerful, empowering programs in there. Yeah, it's all connected and you're right; you've got to have that first.

Tracey Lee: It's the foundation. And we have this mindset, too. We want everything to happen, instant gratification. How quickly can I have abs, how quickly can I be able to look and feel like this? Where did that expectation come from? It came from outside of us, and we gave it all the power and then we expect to meet those expectations. It's like we didn't even really choose them, or maybe we chose them, but we didn't even know why we chose them. They've just been imprinted into our minds to meet unrealistic expectations and then we're setting ourselves up for failure before we even get started.

Leslie Christie: I like to call it mass consciousness. We're giving the power to mass consciousness, not asking ourselves what we want. And a lot of the language, especially today, that has been discussed is what

I talk about all the time. The importance of vision and understanding who you want to show up like every single day. The self-image script is key. When it comes to your wellness, I like to use the term weight release because so much of what we struggle with has to do with emotions and forgiveness and the judgment and the perfectionism that we place on ourselves every single day. We have to start where we're at and just let it go and decide who we want to be every single day and just show up.

Who was the speaker who made the list of their values? Oh my gosh, she was an amazing speaker. She made a list of her core values on her computer and then that's what she looks at every day. Was it Tanya? That is so powerful. But the biggest thing that I teach clients is, first of all, before you do anything, before you sign up for a fitness program or a nutrition program to release weight, you need to get your vision clear first. Because 96% to 98% of everything we do is a subconscious program. I think Debbie mentioned that. And that means that it's like our cell phone. If our apps are slow and they're not working, we don't continue to put new stuff in them. We either upgrade our phone or we fix our phone and we empty it. And it's the same thing with our program. If we're trying to do something new with health or fitness or wellness, but we're still operating with the same phone, what's going to happen? We're not going to get the results we want, right?

Tracey Lee: Yes, absolutely. Even when we change the outside look, like when women quickly lose weight, they haven't accepted the woman who's lost weight. They're still the same woman. That's why they gain it right back. That's the image. That's how that intention in the beginning is going to serve you so well moving forward.

Leslie Christie: Yeah, because if you're still seeing yourself as unhealthy, as unfit, as unmotivated, even if you get quick results, you're just going to go back. It's like the autopilot of the plane. You're going to veer off for turbulence, and you're coming back. So that's why the image is so important. And yes, it's wonderful to move and it's wonderful to clean up your food. But before you do anything, you've got to spend time on what's your vision, who you want to show up as, and if you feel you are worth it, right? To say to yourself, I'm worth the time to think about this and the investment of money. We've been talking about the importance of having to invest in yourself. It's so true. So that's where I start with clients.

Tracey Lee: It's amazing. Everyone's sharing stories here, being vulnerable, and really showing up because that is not always easy to do, but it allows people to feel connected to you. I remember people coming to me at the gym, and they would look at me like I was this superhuman. And I'm thinking, you've no idea. I mean, at the time, I was going through so many things, but I didn't allow myself to be vulnerable. So they didn't really know. And if I had, they probably would have felt a deeper connection to me, but I was afraid to do that at the time. So I want to ask you, can you share your journey of what brought you to doing what you're doing and what your biggest get-out-of-her-own-way moment has been that made a big shift for you?

Leslie Christie: Well, I think it's important to mention that I struggled with weight through the early part of my life, especially into adolescence as we become kind of awkward in that stage. I remember standing on stage for ballet classes and having everyone around me feel like I was the biggest one on the stage. Maybe there are people out there who can relate to that. And that never feels good. I was always interested in that. As I got a little bit older, I would say in my teenage years, I discovered fitness, and I started to work out. I discovered the power of healthy and positive habits and what they can do. But as I got into my later years in my professional career, I realized that it's not about fitness. It's actually about how you look at yourself and the mindset of who you see yourself as. Do you see yourself as this healthy, fit, and energized person, or do you see yourself as someone who's tired and sluggish?

So, for me, that really made a difference. I started my news anchor career, and I wanted to go to the next level with news. I was thinking I'm going to see and I'm going to do all this stuff. So, I hired a coach and realized through that process that I was actually out of line with my true values, which was pumping the world up. Somebody said that they don't listen to the news at all. I get that. I was in the news, and I don't even listen to the news because you become what is around you. Through that process, I realized I was out of step and wasn't where I needed to be. I went back to fitness because I had always been teaching it. I use the principles you're discussing that you did for this summit, like you're just going to connect with something, you're going to do it, and you don't know how, but you're going to do it. I was studying, and I was a Bob Proctor consultant back then. I've been studying this material for probably 17 years, and I just used that to build a business.

Now, I teach women about their mindset. And if they're struggling, it's an opportunity to go deep and really make a shift. It's part of the journey, right? Use that as a catalyst for some real big shifting and not just health and wellness, but it translates into all other areas of your life.

Tracey Lee: Going deep is, from my experience, one of the biggest things, the biggest opportunities that I had to build the strongest foundation to continue stepping into what I am meant to do. We don't realize how surface-level most of us live. We just accepted our first answer. We don't really ask ourselves deeper questions. We don't even give ourselves space to do that because we're so busy. I sit outside, and I just feel the sun on my face. I just close my eyes and take a moment. We've become so accustomed to feeling a certain way, with our bodies, with our minds, with our energy levels, and all of these things, and that's our normal. We don't even know what it feels like to be in a different space. And until you actually take yourself out of it and experience something different, you have no idea. I think that's the power of being with someone like yourself who can help you just experience something you haven't experienced yet, and then discover what your life can look and feel like.

Leslie Christie: There's that lovely metaphor about the fleas in the jar. I don't know if you've heard this, but the fleas are in a jar, and you put a lid on the top. The fleas try to jump out, but they can only go as high as the lid. When you take the lid off, the fleas only jump as high as the lid because they've lived with that lid in their lives for so long. They don't know how to jump out. It's important to know that you can do what you want to do. There are no limitations. This whole I'm getting old, I can't do it, and I can't move. Starting to focus on possibility rather than limitation is a massive shift. Where you put your energy, your focus, that's what's going to grow.

Tracey Lee: A hundred percent, a hundred percent. So, walk me through a client case study. I always focus on the pillars of a holistic life and our health, of course, has to be in there. Your health could be how you take care of your home in terms of toxins. Living a healthy lifestyle can have multiple components. So when someone comes to you as a new client and says I'm ready for a change. What do you look for? How do you walk them through the process? And even before that, what do you think is their biggest obstacle in the beginning that will continue to hold them back if not addressed?

Leslie Christie: Well, there are so many answers to that question, but when I'm working with clients, I see, especially in driven women, that criticism is a big one. That self-judgment piece. Here's what I used to be like: Why can't I do this anymore? If I can't do it 100%, why do it at all? I think the biggest thing to do is to drop judgment and realize where we are now isn't a reflection of our potential, it's just a reflection of all the thoughts we've been thinking to this point. Thoughts really become things. And this is what I teach. Thoughts, equal feelings, equal actions, equal results. You think something, it causes you to feel something. Feeling something causes you to take a certain action, and taking that action gives you certain results.

If you say to yourself, I can never stick to a program. You're like, oh my gosh, I can never do this. You do not feel confident. You feel like you're not going to follow it. And then you're going to, of course, take that action. And what does that person do? Who feels that way? They're probably going to quit. They're going to say, why bother? And then you're not going to get the results. But if you're thinking, I can do this, and you're going to feel empowered. Empowered people take specific actions, and then that's going to give them a certain result. But it's important to know, and I explain this to everybody, that everything we're doing is a program. We have to become aware of that program and then rewire it.

So, to answer your question, the first thing I'd say is let's create a vision, okay? Just like Debbie said, you have to know your goal. You have to know your vision, and you can't let yourself stand in the way of that. You have to get out of your own damn way. You have to think, how do I want to live my life? Do I want to be able to run after my grandkids? What does that look like for me? Do I want to run up the stairs and not feel winded? Do I want to be able to shop in those stores that I've wanted to shop in for so long? And then have the courage to put it down. Once we get that image, we need to do the next step. And that is, what are the stories that I've been telling myself that are getting in the way of my success? So if I'm always saying, "I'm tired," if I'm always saying, "This is never going to work." If I'm always saying I don't like vegetables, those are stories that we tell ourselves, and everything is neutral. It's the spin we put on it. We must be aware of those things, thoughts, and beliefs we tell ourselves. And then we have to change them with some affirmative statements. We have to reprogram the mind. Like we're saying, you read your image script over, and it's the same thing. You have to keep reading it. Space repetition or emotional impact is the only way to change a program or what's known as a paradigm.

Every day you have to put the work into it. That's the work that has to be done along with or before you're taking the other steps. And once you do this, this is the cool thing. We're going to get hits of inspiration as to what's going to work for us because it's not a one-size-fits-all approach. Some people love Pilates, some people love spinning. Some people just like to walk, but until you have your image, you're not going to know what's right for you until you do the work, and then you're going to get hit with inspiration. You know, it might be fasting. It might be being vegan. Everything is different, but you have to do the work first. Otherwise, all we're doing is treating the symptoms but not treating the cause. Kind of like a band-aid approach. So that's part of the process I go through, but the support is needed because the paradigm is really strong. It's going to tell you, "I'm too tired to do this. Why bother?" It's not going to work because that reptilian part of your brain wants to keep you cozy and comfortable. So, you've got to be aware.

Tracey Lee: You have to create a new default pattern, right? And you have to be responsible enough to create that new default. And once you do, you actually will look back and say, I couldn't even be that way if I wanted to anymore. I can't. It's just not even possible. That's a really cool, amazing place to be. But it does take time. It takes perseverance and it takes persistence.

What I've found is that as soon as you shift your perspective on something, all of a sudden, you reclaim your power back. If you've got a perspective that something isn't going to work or, you know, I'm going to try this and I'm probably not going to like it or why bother or, I don't have time because if I do this and this person isn't going to be home in time to make dinner for the kids and on and on—that's just a record player just going around and around. We all have done it; we've all been there, but the only way is to go after each one in its own way and reframe it. I'm going to shift my perspective. And I'm going to use the steps that Leslie's giving me so I can move through this. And then every time you do that, you're like, wow, this is friggin' awesome. You're willing to try other things too. Maybe try that and know that you're your own boss, your own CEO of your queendom. If you don't like it, then don't do it. And it's okay.

Leslie Christie: Yes. Here's the thing, though. If you have a clear vision that you're emotionally involved with, and you're reading that and looking at that every day of the person you want to show up as that's going to motivate you to take action. A lot of times, we're trying to do things without the vision or the emotional why, I like to call, behind us. And that's just not going to fly when you're tired, when work is busy, or when you've got 50,000 things happening. But if I show up as the best version of myself and when I get moving, I raise my vibe or feel more confident. And I know what I give to myself, I'm going to give 100-fold to those around me, and that's going to get you doing what you need to do. The other thing I wanted to mention is this big forgiveness piece. Actually, the beautiful talk the other day about money reminded me of working with your image and weight release because there's a lot of shame and there is a lot of forgiveness needed. One of the gifts that I've got for you is a body appreciation meditation because it can be very helpful to just see your body in a new way. When you walk by the mirror, how many of us do this? I can't look in the mirror, or I don't want to look at myself, or I don't like to look at myself in pictures. Well, we've got to work on that, and we've got to appreciate and start from where we are now to move forward into that next stage. It's got to be from a place of love. We don't want to punish ourselves with exercise or punish ourselves with food deprivation. We want to move from a place of love because that's who we are and that's who we want to show up as. I hope that makes sense.

Tracey Lee: We're disconnected from ourselves, so we put ourselves in a place where we feel we're in comparison mode, but the deeper connected you are to yourself, it helps you create that vision of who you actually are. When I look at people now, I don't look at their exterior. I look at their souls. We're all beautiful souls. We're all connected. I always say we're all sisters here. Your vision will not only serve you. It's going to serve so many other people, too, because your vision is truly who you are. So, the deeper you are connected to yourself, you're going to be able to connect to that vision and create that vision. A vision and purpose can feel heavy, but it's just about how you want to feel.

Leslie Christie: Who do you want to show up as? Yeah, it's worth the time and investment because remember that statistic Debbie shared— 96 to 98 % of all our results are a subconscious program. So, we have to change that program, right? And we have to do that by creating a better program. There's a reason for us to do that; it's worth the time and the investment time to figure that out. It's incredible, this work. I mean, it's done tremendous things for my life.

Tracey Lee: You want to front-load it in a way that isn't just about you doing the gym stuff, it's about front-loading and setting the foundation and the stage. It's like, I'm going to go and cook this beautiful recipe. Well, you're ready; you're in there with your recipe, and you don't have anything in your fridge. Now you have to go and do this. Prepare yourself, get everything unique, and start making your recipe with everything that you need. You're going to feel confident, and you're going to have a stronger foundation because you know it's going to be easier.

Leslie Christie: It's going to be easier.

Tracey Lee: More flow, right? And that is huge. Wow. Yeah, you are a wise woman and have a very beautiful rooted confidence in you, Leslie. I felt that the first time I spoke with you. Obviously, being in this work for 17 years has served you very well, and now you're using it to serve other women. That's just really beautiful.

Leslie Christie: Thank you.

Tracey Lee: What would one thing be that you would just say to a woman who's just getting started? What's one thing you could share?

Leslie Christie: I would say understand that small steps add up big time. We try to overcomplicate things. Take it easy. Take it slow. We have something within our fitness program. We call them WMMs. It's movement, mindset, and water. We need water, right? I would say you start there. You start with water, you hydrate your body, and you get everything working properly. It's the wellness foundation, and then you're just going to move your body, whatever that means to you. I always say to people, it's great if you join our fitness class, but that may not be your jam. So, you get out, you walk, and you go for hikes, whatever works for you. And then, of course, the mindset piece is remembering your vision and understanding that the conversation you have with yourself about yourself when no one is listening creates your results. Are you telling yourself, I'm not worth it, or are you telling yourself, I'm fat? I mean, that's what you think of when your kids are learning to walk. They started to walk, and they fell. You didn't say, what the heck are you doing? Get up. I can't believe you fell. Can't you get it right? You pick them up, and you say, come on, you can do it. Yeah, you are amazing. It's one step at a time. You've got this. And we have to be that way to ourselves because that's what works. It's not the berating. It's not that kind of coaching. It's kindness, it's understanding that resilience and the love behind it make such a difference. So, if anyone can take anything away from that, it takes courage to do anything great in our lives.

Tracey Lee: It takes courage, and encouragement breeds courage. So, encourage yourself all day, every day. You got to be your biggest hero. Someone said that, too. You have to be your biggest hero. I love it. You're amazing. You're not only beautiful, you're so talented, you're wise, you're incredible. I'm so happy that you're in this circle, and I just really appreciate you saying yes to getting out of your own damn way and coming and sharing your wisdom with us.

Thank you, beautiful Bella!

Leslie Christie: Thank you, Tracey.

To watch Tracey Lee's interview with Leslie Christie, scan the QR Code below.

Jenn Iannuzzi

https://www.linkedin.com/in/jenniferiannuzzi/

Jenn Iannuzzi is a dynamic marketing communications professional with over 15 years of experience championing start-ups and established brands in areas ranging from tech and law to therapy and jewelry. A seasoned copywriter, she helps companies find their unique voice and make sure it's heard.

Known for her "roll-up-your-sleeves" approach, Jenn dives deep into every project, transforming complex ideas into clear, engaging messaging that grabs attention. Her knack for storytelling has secured media coverage from heavyweights like *USA Today*, *The New York Times*, *CNN*, and *The Wall Street Journal* — and it's helped her clients achieve sky-high conversion rates from their campaigns.

But what sets Jenn apart is her enthusiasm and authenticity. Whether she's working alongside start-up dreamers or Fortune 500 power players, Jenn gets right to the heart of the client and their customer. You can find her on Instagram @jenniferiannuzzi where she shares the realness of her journey as a Gen X, perimenopausal woman — with candor and a whole lot of laughter.

"I was honestly so humbled to be invited to emcee this incredibly powerful and moving event. I tell stories for a living and was so grateful to help create a safe and welcoming space for Tracey to empower these beautiful women to bring their stories forward."

Tracey Lee

Tracey Lee Living
Business Mindset Coach

https://www.facebook.com/Traceyleeliving/
https://www.instagram.com/traceyleeliving_tll/
https://www.traceyleeliving.com/

Tracey Lee is a Business Mindset Coach whose work extends far beyond conventional business strategy. She assists women in cutting through the noise, confronting the obstacles in their way, and building businesses rooted in their deepest truths. Tracey created SheLeads Ventures for women who are weary of adhering to traditional rules, exhausted from trying to meet everyone's expectations, and ready to carve out their own space and build businesses on their own terms.

Tracey does not subscribe to the notion of wearing all the hats, pretending everything is perfect, or equating "busyness" with success. Women often bear the burden of expectations—juggling everything, maintaining appearances, and smiling through exhaustion. Tracey challenges this approach, believing that acknowledging and addressing what truly holds women back is crucial for progress. This belief led her to establish the *"Get Out of Your Own Damn Way"* movement, which emphasizes that recognizing these barriers is the first step toward moving forward.

In her programs, Tracey helps women reframe their challenges. Instead of feeding the struggle, she encourages addressing it directly, shifting perspectives, and using it as fuel for growth. She guides women to confront their fears, clarify their ideas, and realize that they are the ones meant to bring those ideas to fruition. Her approach is not about following a pre-existing blueprint but creating a plan rooted in one's own truth, leveraging personal strengths, passions, and life circumstances.

Through SheLeads Ventures, Tracey takes women on a journey of self-discovery, leading them to step powerfully into themselves first, and then into their business. Whether a woman is just starting out, feeling stuck, or ready to scale, Tracey meets her where she is and provides guidance every step of the way. She demonstrates how to overcome self-imposed obstacles, reclaim personal power, and build a business that is not only successful but deeply fulfilling.

Having navigated this path herself—through years of building her business, facing failures, investing in mentors, and learning to present her authentic self—Tracey, as a Projector, is naturally adept at seeing potential in women long before they recognize it in themselves. She helps them uncover that potential and guides them in making decisions that advance them toward their vision with confidence and clarity.

Working with Tracey is not just about starting a business; it is about personal transformation, stepping into greatness, and understanding that one possesses everything needed to create the desired impact, life, and business. She is dedicated to helping women tap into their power, stand out, and unapologetically claim their space.

This is Tracey's mission, and she invites others to join her at the table or create their own. The world needs more women embracing their full potential and building businesses that genuinely reflect who they are.

Conclusion

As you close the pages of this book, I hope you feel the power and inspiration these remarkable conversations offer. Each story is a testament to the strength, vulnerability, and resilience these incredible women have shown as they've risen above their circumstances to make a meaningful impact on their own terms.

If you want to truly experience the essence of what transpired at the Get Out Of HER Own Damn Way Summit, I invite you to visit my YouTube channel, "Get Out Of HER Own Damn Way." The "HER" represents that inner part of you that knows you have everything it takes to go all the way. There, you can watch each interview and immerse yourself in the full depth of these transformative conversations.

My name is Tracey Lee, founder of Traceyleeliving Coaching. I am dedicated to empowering women to discover, embrace, and live their truth. Through the "Get Out of Your Own Damn Way" movement, I've created coaching programs designed to help you uncover your superpowers and realize that you can BE, DO, and HAVE anything you desire, regardless of age, circumstances, or past experiences.

At the heart of my coaching philosophy is the principle of "Know Yourself, Build Your Business." I'm here to help you tap into your inner wisdom, harness the resilience you've developed, and turn your visions into actionable plans. My SheLeads Ventures Coaching programs are specifically designed to support women as they plant their flags and create fulfilling, successful businesses.

You can find more information about my coaching programs, resources, and how to work with me at Traceyleeliving.com. Join our vibrant community, access valuable tools, and start your journey of transformation.

Thank you for exploring these inspiring stories with me. May they motivate you to step into your own power, embrace your truth, and build a life and business that truly resonates with who you are.

Sending you all my love and light,
Tracey Lee

Join the Wave.

Women in midlife are choosing their next chapter on their terms, harnessing decades of wisdom, triumphs, and resilience to create businesses that are life-giving for themselves and those they serve.

Tracey Lee, founder of Traceyleeliving Coaching, inspires women and girls globally to find, love, and live their truth. By uncovering hidden talents, shattering glass ceilings, and breaking through barriers, these women build businesses from their most powerful selves. They are disrupting industries, making the world a better place, and coming together in sisterhood.

A new movement is born. Women in midlife are planting their flags and creating successful businesses, proving to be unstoppable.

Tracey Lee started the Get Out of Your Own Damn Way movement, which is at the heart of everything she teaches, creates, and lives. Her SheLeads Ventures Coaching programs will guide you step-by-step to uncover your superpower, helping you believe that you can BE, DO, and HAVE anything you want in life. Age, circumstances, and your past do not define you; they propel you to become more.

Looking to step into your next career with you at the helm, creating a business that is meaningful and fulfilling?

Come check out all Tracey Lee has to offer to support you on your journey:

Website: https://www.traceyleeliving.com/
Instagram: https://www.instagram.com/traceyleeliving_tll/
Facebook: https://www.facebook.com/Traceyleeliving/

www.ingramcontent.com/pod-product-compliance
Lightning Source LLC
Chambersburg PA
CBHW071320120626
46546CB00002B/384